BEFORE
THE BATTLE

BEFORE THE BATTLE

A Commonsense Guide to
Leadership and Management

**LT. Gen. Edward M. Flanagan, Jr.
U.S. Army (Ret.)**

PRESIDIO

Published by Presidio Press, 31 Pamaron Way, Novato, CA 94947

Library of Congress Cataloging in Publication Data

Flanagan, E. M., 1921–
  Before the battle.

  1. Command of troops. 2. Leadership. 3. United States.
Army—Personnel management. I. Title.
UB210.F54   1984   355.3'3041   84-15960
ISBN 0-89141-210-7

Permission has been granted by *Army* magazine to reprint the following articles which originally appeared in that publication: "All
in the Name of Efficiency Reports," copyright June 1982; "At
War with the Dictionary," copyright June 1977 ("Communications"); "Boss, Relations With," copyright September 1977;
"Rescue," copyright July 1978.

Drawings in text by Joseph L. Sinnott
Printed in the United States of America

TO MY WIFE, PEG

Contents

DISPOSITION FORM

For use of this form, see AR 340-15; the proponent agency is TAGO.

REFERENCE OR OFFICE SYMBOL	SUBJECT
ISBN: 0-89141-210-7	Success in the Military

TO All Leaders   **FROM** Kane/883-1373   **DATE** 15 Mar 85   CMT 1

Leadership can be learned from A through Z — or in this case, **A**dministration through **W**ives.

LTG Edward M. Flanagan, Jr., USA (Ret.) has written *Before the Battle* with a single objective in mind: to help *you* succeed as a leader. His method is not complicated, but it is practical. And, more important, it works!

The desired result of all military training is success in combat. Before you and your troops face that monumental challenge, however, you will have many problems on a different level to solve. They may not be as dramatic, but they are of fundamental importance.

Start at the beginning, Administration, and proceed to the forty-three commandments in the Summary. Apply these lessons and you will succeed before the battle.

Be Military; Be Ready for War, and you will Win.

Robert V. Kane
Publisher
Presidio Press

DA FORM AUG 80 **2496**   PREVIOUS EDITIONS WILL BE USED   ☆ U.S. G.P.O.

Introduction

1. The most important precept of leadership that I know is that one can learn how to be a leader. Nonetheless, some men and women are born leaders—or so it seems.

2. Everyone knows men and women who seem to sense, instinctively, exactly the right way to get a group to do willingly and efficiently what they want. Napoleon, the grand strategist, was a leader —witness the unbelievable devotion of his Guard—first a platoon and, finally, a whole corps—to him, the emperor. He was a general so young (a brigadier at twenty-four) that one would almost have to conclude that he was born with the traits that made it possible for him to assemble and lead an army of men to the gates of Moscow under the most intolerable circumstances of weather, roads, health, and terrain. That takes leadership. But for every one of these intuitive, charismatic leaders—the Alexanders, Napoleons, Vince Lombardis, Jim Gavins, and John F. Kennedys—there must be twenty other successful men and women who have *learned* the principles of leadership.

3. My aim is to put down in one place the things I have learned about military leadership, organization, management, and operations, spelled out in words that make my meaning clear. My thoughts run the gamut from administration to wives—God bless them. To make this book easy to read and ideas easy to find, I have simply lined up the topics in alphabetical order and listed them in the Table of Contents, which thus doubles in brass (no pun intended) as the index. Each thought or idea is relatively short— reading time no more than six or seven minutes at the most.

4. At first glance, some of the topics in the Table of Contents may seem completely foreign and irrelevant to the business on hand: leadership. But leadership, basically, is simply getting men

and women to do a job well, economically, and willingly. In this context, then, items such as communications, desk drawers, messages, telephones, and three-by-five cards fall into place because they discuss various ways, means, and methods that help you do your job better, more carefully, more successfully, with the interests of your troops at heart whenever that is possible (which should be almost always). All the items in the book strive to do one thing primarily: make you a more successful leader. The results of that achievement are twofold: One, you satisfy your inner self, you build your self-confidence, and you make yourself worthy in your own eyes; but, secondly and perhaps more importantly, your success means a better unit, a better Army, and a better country. Each chapter, then, seeks to be yet another piece of the whole—like the pieces of a jigsaw puzzle, all of which are needed to make a complete picture.

5. Leadership is complicated. It always has been. Each generation has different problems, aspirations, motivations. There's much more to leadership than simply moving a squad or a division from Point A to Point B. If you're that rare bird, a natural leader, don't bother to read on. But if you're one of the majority who must work at it, this is for you. Leaders must work to learn their trade.

6. Closely akin to leadership is management. There have been many tomes written on the subject of management and its various aspects: MBO (management by objective), management by exception, management by committee, management by chiefs, management by workers, and so on, *ad nauseam*. In my quest to learn what I could on the subject of management, I asked many of the so-called experts to give me their definition of the word. The answers were as numerous as the responders. But after a great deal of talking, questioning, and thinking on the subject, I decided that this is the best definition: "the way to get things done." It follows that good management, which is the elusive pot of gold at the end of the manager's rainbow, is simply the way to get things done better, smarter, easier, cheaper, quicker.

7. Having decided that, my awe of the management types, whose jargon is as esoteric as that of social scientists, comptrollers, and logisticians, began to decrease somewhat, and I began to think of the ways that we do things in the military—specifically in the

Army. I decided that our proven leadership principles were every bit as good, and perhaps better than, the complicated principles of management (as practiced in the civilian sector) that I had found so hard to understand. And now that I'm retired from the Army and have held a management job in a civilian firm for nearly six years, I know this for certain: The military is head and shoulders above civilians in both management and leadership.

8. There have been many books written on the subject of leadership. And there's an obvious question: If the Army and the military have been so successful in devising, developing, disseminating, and determining the principles of leadership, why another book on the subject? Here are my reasons:

a. I feel that in this era of the so-called MVA (modern volunteer Army) many of the old precepts of leadership have been diluted, confused, and bad-mouthed by otherwise well-intentioned senior leaders, seemingly in order to make the Army comfortable for the volunteer and thus to attract more recruits and retain those we have. Thus, some of our young lieutenants and NCOs are—at least—confused about their roles in the Army, about discipline, morale, and troop welfare. Because of the confusion, there is necessarily much indecision. I feel we need to clear the air and "get our heads on straight," as our young soldiers might say. "The harder right instead of the easier wrong" is still the correct way of doing things, but we may have sacrificed the "harder right" because of expediency and the need to create an MVA.

b. There is confusion about the new words of management: productivity, work-measurement, goal-analysis, problem solving, decision making, and a host of other complex phrases covering old and simple ideas. These terms need to be put into their proper context and perspective.

c. Civilians do not understand how we do things in the military. They think that officers in general and generals in particular are either unapproachable, flint-hearted martinets, or ambitious, ruthless despots whose sole motivations are self-aggrandizement, personal power, and advancement. I might possibly be able to give them some insight into the heart of the Army, a heart that pumps a steady flow of concern about the problems of our troops, the needs of the country, and the desire to do something constructive for both.

    d. The things I am going to say are not original with me. They are a distillation of the thoughts, ideas, and practices of many of the splendid leaders under whom, and with whom, I have served over the years. I hope that I have been able to assemble in one place their words and example and pass them on to the next generation of the Army's leaders.

    9. In my view, the Army cannot be a civilian organization with a military mission. In brutal reality, we in the military must face the fact that we are training men to fight, to kill, and to avoid being killed themselves. We are not training men to produce yet another, flashier model in a long series of cars from Detroit, a better cereal, or a better mousetrap. What we are doing is far more fundamental and far more important. We are training men to defend the United States, to preserve for all its citizens what all of us accept, deserve, and own—our God-given and Constitution-guaranteed rights. Ours is a difficult profession; it is a vocation, a calling to which not everyone is adaptable. But in my view, it is the most important job in the country. Its importance transcends that of manufacturing, law, sales, architecture, and other professions, because it is the insurance, the security, the protection, for all else. An army cannot be a sometime thing; it must be full-time, it must be tough, lean, disciplined, well-trained, and ready to fight. And we cannot have that kind of army on a part-time, eight-to-five basis with leaders only partially dedicated and improperly motivated. It's got to be "all the way," as they say in the airborne units.

    10. And so for these reasons, *Before the Battle* came into being. I believe the ideas I have assembled may be as applicable to the problems of civilian management as they are to military leadership. They are as pertinent to the junior NCO as they are to our most important leader, who, in these years of peace, is any troop commander.

    11. I've tried out these ideas and they have worked for me. I hope they will work for you and help you to have the finest unit of its kind and size in the Army. Then the Army and the country wins.

    12. If I seem at times dogmatic—even reactionary—it is because

I feel that a return to some of our time-proven and battle-tested precepts is in order. Or as one of my football-oriented brigade commanders used to say, "Let's get back to basic blocking and tackling."

The ultimate command post, the Pentagon. U.S. Army photo

Reduce
Eliminate
Simplify
Consolidate
Unload
Eradicate

Administration

It is no accident, of course, that the words above spell out, perhaps painfully, an acronym—RESCUE. The administration of the Army is in dire need of just that—RESCUE. Any company commander, first sergeant, or company clerk who has been on the job for more than a month can recite in frustrating detail the regulations, the reports, the files, the rosters, the sometimes bewildering paperwork connected with administering and commanding today's company —the lowest level unit in the Army with both tactical and administrative responsibilities.

A study by the Administration Center at Fort Benjamin Harrison unearthed a total of 283 separate administrative tasks performed at one time or another by some or all of the Army's companies. These included:

> morning reports
> strength reports
> supply files
> requisitions for repair parts
> reports of survey
> daily materiel readiness reports
> signature headcount sheets
> deadline reports
> survey rosters
> personnel data cards
> letters of indebtedness
> charge sheets
> training highlight report
> duty rosters

The study also looked at the root causes for the clerks and the company commanders spending so much of their time with paperwork. The study listed the following among the principal evils:

inexperienced clerks

CYA (in military jargon, Cover Your Backside)

diminished authority at the company level

staff-generated nonessential requirements

excessive typing and retyping

siphoning of trained men to do other jobs

excessive requirements by commanders up the chain for more and more details on all operations

(This last may have started back in the Korean War; toward the end of the war, the Army headquarters was monitoring the actions of platoon leaders.)

That's the situation at the company level. (There are now personnel sections at battalion to handle a lot of this work, but the rules I will give are still applicable.) Administration gluts the channels of the Army (and most big business at all levels); unfortunately, like taxes, it is a necessary evil. One must pay, promote, assign, train, command, feed, clothe, discipline, and account for his men; one must requisition repair parts and maintain his equipment; one must report on his state of readiness to higher headquarters. How to unshackle the company and other commanders from their wearying, time-consuming, burdensome paper chain? How free the various levels of staff and command of the administrative trappings that clog the system, swell the payroll, and crowd the office space? Here are a few ideas and suggestions:

1. Decentralize decision making as far as possible (company and battalion commanders are usually pretty smart). This is undoubtedly the most important and effective step we can take to cut down the paperwork. This rule definitely applies at the battalion and company levels. It's another way of saying have faith and confidence in your subordinates.

2. Permit the company commander and first sergeant to do their paperwork in longhand—particularly paperwork involving troops as individuals—and require battalion headquarters to process the papers.

3. Consolidate all reports possible; eliminate duplicate ones.

4. Review reports requirements frequently to make certain they

are still valid. (A staff officer may put a requirement on units for a report on a periodic basis and then forget to turn it off.)

5. Cut down on the number of copies of paperwork. Extra copies serve only to clutter up file cabinets and involve staff officers who really have no business in the action in the first place. As a corollary, though, make certain that the action officer who must work on an action gets a copy as soon as possible.

6. Permit some memos to be written in longhand. There's no need to have perfect copies of memos even if you are a general or a senior staff officer at a high level. Develop a clear hand so the person who gets your memo can read it without a handwriting expert for guidance. Writing longhand also cuts down on excess verbiage. (Incidentally, if we required all routine radio communications to be written out on a message pad and transmitted via Morse code, we'd soon cut down on the pollution of our communications channels and simplify our radio gear. But that's another subject.)

7. Cut down on files. Go through them ruthlessly and throw away the excess. It's amazing how infrequently one is called upon to produce the deathless prose written only a week ago. Some files are necessary, but they must be current and useful—not an archive for posterity and one's ego.

8. At the higher levels, set up staff services organizations (not steno pools, a title that stenos apparently loathe) to centralize dictation, typing, filing, and other necessary administration. There's no need for everyone—not even generals and top echelon staff officers—to have his own private secretary. Discover how fast it is to place your own phone calls. The response at the other end is equally fast—particularly if one is of fairly high rank. This eliminates all the jazz about which senior officer or other official gets on the phone first. (I know one general who answers his own phone, saying: "This is Brigadier General ———. May I help you?" For a very busy man, however, this may be impossible.)

9. Consolidate and centralize references. Some action officers need to have ready reference to statistics and reports they use frequently. Okay. Let them have them; that saves time. But eliminate the rabbit warrens of file cabinets and bookcases that action officers often set up for themselves. Have a complete set of files cen-

trally located so everyone in a section or division can use them. Space is at a premium in offices everywhere—particularly the Pentagon and similar headquarters.

10. Cull out the inconsequential detail that is cosmetic and not substantive. (This will require staff officers and commanders occasionally to admit, "I don't know," to some picayune question.)

11. Have faith in your subordinates. Action officers often know more about a given subject than their bosses. If they don't, they should be fired. (One high ranking and understanding general said that he'd accept being surprised by something he read first in the *Washington Post*. He insisted on pushing decision making down to the level that could best handle it. In other words, he tried to shift the detailed problem solving and decision making out of Washington.)

12. Give your subordinate room to operate, to make honest mistakes, to learn through experience. Company commanders, for example, do not start out from day one as full-blown, mature, totally competent commanders.

13. Eliminate "nit-picking" up the chain. This means that the layers of management through which a paper passes must be willing to accept minor administrative errors provided the substance is sound. It means using a "working draft" instead of a final paper at each layer. (Speaking of layers, General Abrams, the late, great Chief of Staff, used to call action officers direct to his office. He asked one of them how long it took him to get there. The officer, a lieutenant colonel, said that it was a five-minute walk, but that, because of the layers of colonels and generals he had to pass through before reaching the Chief, it took him an hour. Needless to say, General Abrams promptly put a stop to that. The inevitable sequel is, however, that it then took the colonel an hour to get back to his desk, debriefing all the way down the line. This is also true at the battalion level—albeit to a lesser extent.)

14. Emphasize the important; de-emphasize procedures and formality. What I'm proposing is simply this: Put authority back where it belongs and eliminate all the unnecessary reports and justifications. In World War II, for example, as a battery commander, I could bust my first sergeant and select another of my buck ser-

geants to become the first sergeant. Today, those acts require a board at Department of Army level. But somehow we mucked through and won World War II.

Now that a battalion commander has an administrative center to handle all his battalion's paperwork, he is in a perfect position to ease the burden on his company commanders by implementing some or all of the suggestions I've just made.

And while we're on the subject of administration at the lower levels, consider the duty roster. A few rules apply here: (1) The duty roster is NCO business, but the commander must be aware of its execution; (2) the number of duty-exempt soldiers must be minimal; (3) the changes to the duty roster after it is published must be few and far between; (4) the roster must be published well in advance, so that soldiers can plan their off-duty time; (5) the roster must be meticulously and equitably kept, so that all duties are spread out fairly and evenly.

Another important point in the administration of the company and battalion has to do with the selection of the best NCOs for the key company slots. One battalion commander violates the "decentralization" rule to the extent of approving company commanders' choices of company training NCOs. The battalion CO makes certain that the best squad leaders or fire team leaders are selected for these extremely important slots. Obviously the entire company benefits when the best NCOs are in positions of companywide rather than limited squad or platoon influence.

Company or battery punishment is often unevenly applied from unit to unit. I tried to solve the problem in my battalion by setting up a battalion hard-labor platoon under a senior, well-qualified disciplinarian of an NCO who was on full-time duty in the position.

Before I established a hard-labor platoon, the execution of hard labor in the battalion was left up to the battery commanders. During the so-called hard-labor hours, I noticed a lot of loafing, slow window washing, and lethargic battery area policing by the men assigned extra duty for minor infractions of the rules of good order and discipline (below-standard appearance at inspections, tardiness for formation, improper uniform, short absences, etc.). Therefore, I decided to centralize (in spite of my distaste for centralization) the extra duty at battalion level. Each evening, the men on battalion punishment assembled for extra training. It consisted generally of full field layouts in the battery streets followed by an inspection, a repacking of the full field gear, and then a march of sufficient length under full field to use up the four hours of extra training that day. In addition, when the battalion went to the firing range for a week of firing each month, the hard-labor platoon marched out and back—a distance of some twenty-six miles. I must say that as the months went on, the hard-labor platoon strength dwindled almost to the vanishing point, and the battalion enjoyed good order and military discipline.

Admittedly, I have hit on many rules in the preceding paragraphs. I suppose one could say that they boil down to these: At all levels, curb administrative requirements, minimize reports, and accent only the necessities. (The good commander is the one who knows what these necessities are.)

Athletics, Auto Repair Shops, Hobby Shops

No one has really disproved the above cliché because it's true: A soldier needs activities to fill his off-duty time. (And I don't mean "happy hour" at the NCO or EM Club.) Sports at the company level, for example, involve many men and increase unit esprit by encouraging competition. Spectators turn out for company-level sports because the men on the teams are their buddies. Company-level sports are personal; they're healthful, morale-building, relatively inexpensive (T-shirts with the unit number or nickname do not break the bank), and well worth the time to organize schedules, get equipment, and conduct training and practice. It also helps the officers to know their men and keeps them away from their own "happy hours."

Equally beneficial toward keeping men happy and occupied during off-duty time are hobby shops of all kinds and, particularly in these days when practically every soldier owns at least one car, automotive repair shops. There, at greatly reduced prices, men can buy repair parts and do all kinds of work from simple tune-ups to complete overhauls.

At one point in the Army's history, during the late unlamented days of VOLAR, the Department of Army permitted commanders to authorize the use of their own military motor shops for soldiers during their off-duty time. They were required to pay for repair parts, but they could borrow the unit tools and, in the better organized shops, there was a mechanic on duty to help the troops with their repairs. It may be that the Army still permits this seemingly gross violation of Army Regulations. A commander must have received DA permission—naturally.

During the VOLAR days, I was the commander of the First Infantry Division and Fort Riley. I thought it would be a great morale booster to open the motor shops to the troops for use in repairing their own POVs. Unfortunately, I took DA at its word and sought DA approval. It was an unfortunate move because a civilian bureaucrat in the DCSLOG office was the action officer on my request. Even though he knew that the request was approvable, he loaded the authorization with so many restrictions that I said, "The hell with it," and proceeded to do it my way anyway. I don't advocate that kind of a reaction to a DA directive, but I feel that when you're right, proceed. Be prepared to own up when someone calls your hand, however, and be prepared for the consequences.

Skydiving, motorcycling, hot-rodding, and flying clubs are equally beneficial. Almost any installation has room and facilities for these activities. Again, as the Fort Riley commander, I was frustrated and thwarted when I tried to build a drag-racing strip; the cost was prohibitive. I solved the problem rather easily: I simply closed down the post airfield on Saturday and Sunday afternoons and permitted the troops to drag race to their hearts' content— under competent supervision, of course. At the other end of the field, the skydiving club was jumping from helicopters. Meanwhile, on the back forty, the motorcyclists were roaring up, down, and around a cross-country course set up near some field artillery firing points. None of these activities cost DA or Fort Riley much money. And the troops loved them.

Keeping the troops busy during off-duty hours is particularly important in remote areas where families are not present. In Korea, for example, one division commander scheduled all-night rock concerts for the first evening of any three-day weekend. This kind of activity has a double purpose: The troops are not in trouble in the local "ville," and the commanders know where their men are. The commander of the 2d Division in Korea also placed great emphasis on physical training and athletics: Four-mile runs each morning, Tae kwon do training, and combat football, a sport that is loosely organized mayhem. But the soldiers were happy, occupied, and tired by evening.

(There can be a bit of a problem with this theory. When I commanded a parachute artillery battalion—the DS battalion of the

187th Airborne RCT in Japan—after we had returned from Korea in 1953, very few of the men had their wives and families with them. Consequently, the temptations and enticements of a certain segment of the female population of nearby Kumamoto were so magnetic as to be overpowering for some of the troops. I attempted to keep down the VD rate by working the men so hard during the day with rugged PT and long, rigorous training that they would be exhausted by nightfall and ready only for their own sacks—in barracks. The system worked for a while, but after a couple of months, the battalion was in such good physical shape that it could engage in both activities with nonchalant ease. I was forced to work on the VD problem—the battalion's rate was so high it was known as the "lovers of the regiment"—by other means.)

The point is this: A soldier is theoretically on duty twenty-four hours a day. He trains during duty hours. (He also educates himself; see Education.) But afterwards, he needs things to do for his own welfare and that of his family. The only limitation is the imagination of his commander—and himself. (A commander can set up all kinds of activities, but getting a soldier to participate is another problem.)

Today's society is sports-oriented. Heroes from the athletic fields and courts abound. The new elite are the multimillion-dollar salaried professionals in football, baseball, basketball, and tennis, to name just a few.

Gone are the days of expensive, division-level athletics with full-time team members, trainers, coaches, and managers. But, still, they had their benefits.

One of the most glamorous examples of division-level sports was the football rivalry of the various large units (divisions and corps) during the occupation of Japan shortly after the end of World War II. The 11th Airborne Division, the "Angels," was filled with an uncommonly large number of athletes because airborne attracted the jocks—then, as now. The division had a football team that beat every other team in sight—including a team from our next higher headquarters, 9th Corps, 106 to zip, even though the second half was played by the 11th's bench-sitters, including the team doctor, trainer, and dentist. The division's teams were so good and so victorious that *Stars and Stripes* headlined one victory: "Ho-Hum, It's the Angels Again."

The big day for the 11th's football team came when it was challenged by the Navy in a game to be played in Shanghai. The Navy loaded its team with recent Annapolis football stars from all over the fleet. The Angels went with what they had. Needless to say (or I wouldn't be reporting this episode), the 11th won.

In Europe during the early sixties, division-level sports were still in vogue. The men on the teams were full-time TDY, the coaches were the best that could be recruited from all over the theater, and the equipment and personnel costs were enormous. The demise of that level of sports activities came for a number of reasons: Division commanders started raiding the replacement depots, not for radar operators or tank drivers or even riflemen, but for the best athletes they could find; units were so scattered that only a relatively few men from nearby units could attend; and only a few highly talented soldiers got a part of the action.

The wise and understanding commander puts the sports orientation of today's soldiers to work—for him and his unit. Instead of the division or large unit teams, the best bet is company and battery-level sports. More men (and women) get to play; a fierce competition builds up and, with it, unit esprit and morale. Besides that, a battalion commander can organize his own schedules, set his own times, and control the entire operation. He has built-in competition within his command.

Today, Army posts are well equipped for all kinds and levels of sports. (Fort Bragg, North Carolina, even boasts an indoor ice-skating rink.) Most posts have a number of football and softball fields, and basketball, tennis, squash, and racquetball courts. One of the best sports for company-level activity is soccer because not much equipment is needed, the field is simple to lay out, the rules are easy to learn, and the troops can rough it without fear of many injuries.

My last foray into organized sports came not as a lieutenant colonel but as a lieutenant general. I was the deputy commander of Eighth Army, and the CG, a full general, wanted an Eighth Army hockey team organized. At a staff conference one day, he asked about the progress of the team, the formation of which he had at least suggested rather directly some months before. He had assumed his suggestion had the force of an order. The G–1 somewhat shamefacedly admitted that no progress had been made; he had not even located an officer-in-charge. The CG was understandably miffed. With complete disregard for my own well-being and with a naiveté and confidence born of three stars, I sounded off and said that someplace in the theater there must be an officer who had some experience with ice hockey. Why, I jabbered, even I had played hockey at West Point. Five seconds later, I was the officer-in-charge of the Eighth Army hockey team, much to the relief of the G-1 and the obvious amusement of the rest of the staff.

The G-1 was not, however, off the hook. In no time at all, at my insistent prodding, he had located an officer who had been a hockey coach in his former life, had culled the units for ex-hockey players, and had rounded up from somewhere enough uniforms to get the team geared up. I was amazed to find that many of the ex-hockey players, myself included, had stashed away in their kit bags hockey skates and gloves. And so was founded rapidly and in good order the Eighth Army hockey team. There was, however, only one hockey rink in all of Seoul for all the local teams, so I found myself up at 0600 many Saturday mornings skating with the team and encouraging them. Fortunately, with a couple of KATUSAs (Korean soldiers assigned to the U.S. Army in Korea) who had played hockey for some of the bigger Korean universities, we had a winning team in the local college league.

One of the most memorable and gratifying awards that I have received, more heartening than some medals I have been awarded, was presented to me by the soldier who was the captain of that Eighth Army hockey team. It was a jacket with "UNC Hockey Team" embroidered on the right pocket, "Hockey 6" on the other, and "OIC" above a pair of crossed hockey sticks on the sleeve. I still wear it proudly. Soldiers are great; a commander who does something for them is repaid a thousandfold.

The possibilities for off-duty activities are endless. I knew one battalion commander who could organize events and keep his men stirred up with a plethora of stunts and feats. Not only did he keep the athletes busy, but he organized for the less active troops such diverse entertainments as chess matches, photo displays, card games, and other off-the-wall enterprises. But, most importantly, he also managed to keep the soldiers MOS-qualified and to pass his unit tests.

All of this may seem a distraction from the main objective of training a unit for its primary mission. Naturally, I advocate no such thing. A unit's first goal must always be its combat-readiness —without question. But there comes a time when a unit must relax, and that's when the athletics, the hobby shops, the competitions come into play. To paraphrase an old saying: All work and no play may make a dull unit. A unit's combat-readiness consists of two elements: *(a)* its military proficiency derived from well-trained troops and well-maintained equipment, and *(b)* its morale and esprit. The latter stems in good part from the former.

As in any other endeavor, in athletics the company or battalion commander is the general manager. He must support the program, or it will never succeed to the full measure it could and should. Leadership applies to an athletic and recreation program in the same way it applies to first-class training—commitment, support, and execution.

An example of how leadership and athletics combine is obvious in the 4/325th Airborne BCT stationed in Vicenza, Italy. The BCT has a tackle football team in the Northern Italy football league. As the XO says, "It's a good team—undefeated last season. The battalion commander's philosophy is simple—the cost of membership on the team is quality soldiering. He fired six team members last year for misconduct during the season. Mind you, it was not UCMJ-type misconduct, but it was below the standards of the 4/325th. The team members were not reinstated." And, it seems clear, that's how one develops a good football team *and* a good battalion.

Another successful program that the 4/325th has instituted is the quarterly competition day. Each man in the battalion participates, and may play only one sport. It is a duty day for all troops. Family members may not attend. And according to the XO, "It is good for morale, and it helps our physical training program by adding spice."

In the pre-World War II Army, polo was a sport played on many posts—even infantry posts—on a Sunday or Wednesday afternoon. With the passing of the horse artillery and mounted cavalry, polo went the way of Sam Browne belts. I was at a briefing in the Pentagon one day in the late fifties when Gen. James Gavin proposed to the Chief of Staff, Gen. Maxwell Taylor, that, now that polo was passé in the Army, we needed a new, exciting sport to take its place. His recommendation: skydiving. Jacques Isteau, the civilian who had had so much to do with introducing skydiving in the United States, was the briefer. With General Gavin, the former wartime commander of the 82d Airborne Division, making such a proposal to General Taylor, the former wartime commander of the 101st Airborne Division, there was little doubt of the outcome. The decision: approved and, with it, permission to use Army aircraft to support the sport.

Soldiering and athletics have always gone hand in hand. One supports the other. The perceptive leader combines them successfully.

Physical fitness

*The human brain is still the best computer
ever developed.*

Automatic Data Processing

If the proliferation of ADP on the battlefield and in administration
continues at the tremendous rate of expansion of the past few years,
pretty soon we will have eliminated from decision making the only
computer that can really reason and think—the human brain.

There is definitely a place for automation (one does wonder,
however, how we won World War II without it); the Army's pay
system proves that (see Pay). But a well-trained reconnaissance
unit, using human eyes and ears and brains, is far better than any
sensor system ever built.

Just for openers, consider the relevant value of the so-called
McNamara Line across the border between the Vietnams. We scattered, planted, and sprayed millions of dollars worth of sensors
along VC and NVA trails, near assembly areas, and in supply
dumps. We built an elaborate center with computers and electronic
gadgets to read out the results. Yet I daresay that well-trained men,
using their eyes, ears, brains, and occasionally noses, gathered
more reliable intelligence than any of the sophisticated, expensive
sensors. (Even photo reconnaissance had a hard time penetrating
the jungle to find VC hideouts.)

This does not mean to suggest that automatic data processors
are worthless or not cost-effective. The automation of Army pay
has saved the Army millions of dollars per year by finding and correcting errors, particularly in allotments, that manual systems simply could not discover. And the automation of personnel records is
correcting administrative errors of all sorts.

What I am suggesting is a hard look at the uses to which automation is put. We can go too far. Human judgment, particularly on
the battlefield, can never be subordinated to or dominated by a

machine. The machine must be the slave, not the master. There must be human oversight and override built into any system.

During World War II, the Army made a valiant if vain effort to automate its personnel records—even if through a manual, non-electronic system.

In those days, when artillery lieutenants were still being taught the Morse code, when the duty uniform for officers training their units was starched khakis, and when we were jumping T-5 parachutes (with an opening shock that rattled your molars and made you get into the proper body position the next time) out of C-47s, each soldier's personnel record was typed onto a form made from heavy, stiff paper, almost cardboard, about eight by eleven. Around the four margins of the record were holes numbered to correspond to the items of data included in the record. Thus, a soldier's rank might be #5, his religion #8, his military status #9, and his marital status #22. Obviously, there had to be a number of holes for each item. When the personnel clerk entered an item on the record, he cut open the hole in the margin corresponding to the proper number. The record was then returned to the file box.

When someone wanted to know something about a unit, which men were married, who were the RAs in the unit, which men were corporals, the clerk stuck a long needle, like a knitting needle, through the hole corresponding to the item, and the records whose holes had not been punched out were picked up by the needle going through the proper hole in all the records. And, voilà, there were the proper records clinging to the prod.

Theoretically the system should have worked. In practice, like so many other ideas that work well under ideal laboratory conditions, this one fell on hard times when put to the test in the field. Reasons: The records' edges became rapidly frayed; after a few weeks you know everything about everybody in a company-sized unit anyway (a man generally stayed in the same unit for the duration unless he was cadred out and then he stayed in the next unit for the duration—and that, incidentally, was a valuable lesson of which we lost sight during Korea and to a far greater extent during the Vietnam affair); and the clerks lost the hand-held punch for cutting out the holes.

What happens at the field artillery battalion fire direction center when its generator gets knocked out? How then does it compute fire commands? To paraphrase the old airplane designer as he watched his aircraft crash into a field: "Well, back to the old firing chart."

To think that all of our battlefield computers will always work smoothly, uninterruptedly, and as planned is wishful thinking of the most dangerous kind. In the environment of Vietnam, where we fought an enemy without aircraft to get at our bases and without enough artillery to knock out our base camps routinely, computers worked (at least they kept operating). But on the European battlefield, or on any battlefield against an enemy equipped with nuclear weapons, massive conventional weapons and jammers of all types, computers and their data links will be in constant jeopardy.

Besides that reason for not depending on computers, does a commander need all the information they generate? A vast amount of information that gets into the channels going upward is indigestible by the time it reaches the top. And how accurate is that information when a young trooper at the company level, perhaps in a very hostile area, is feeding the original data into the system with the proverbial stubby pencil?

And so I say: Hold it. Take a good look at what we're doing. Review all those items the Combined Arms Center is putting into the ADP system. Go back to a zero base. Do we really need all that data? Does the commander really need this or that piece of information to make a fast, hard battlefield decision? Be realistic. The next incoming round may knock out your generator, too.

Battalion and company commanders on the battlefields of the future may well be equipped with TV cameras and monitors. Obviously, this would incline the faint-hearted commander to monitor the battle from the safety of a dug-in CP or armored vehicle. This simply cannot be allowed to happen. The commanders at battalion level or below (and, of course, division and brigade commanders) who do not get out to see what is going on have no feel whatever for the difficulties, the hazards, the living conditions of their troops on the line or wherever they may be. They cannot command from a CP—even with ADP, TV, and computer printouts.

A computer printout can tell a commander what his deadline

rate is, it can tell him the status of his repair parts, it can keep him abreast of his rations, personnel strength, awards, casualties, ammunition stocks, and requisition delays. It can feed him operational and intelligence data. But a computer printout can never tell him anything about the morale of his troops, about their well-being, about their urgent needs. A printout or a TV display can tell a commander of the numbers of enemy troops and their general disposition, but it can never tell him anything about their leadership, their drive, their courage, and their determination.

A battalion commander can certainly use a computer for many of the administrative tasks of running his battalion. He can use it for part of his operational decision making. But the computer will never replace his own eyes and ears for determining the facts. It will not replace his own in-house computer, his brain, for weighing all those facts, for leading him through the subjective and objective analyses of his estimate of the situation, and for miraculously processing all that data into a workable decision.

The human brain is still the best computer. In spite of previously unimagined progress in computer technology, only a human's built-in computer can reason and think.

An AWOL soldier is a man with a problem.

AWOL

Throughout the history of the Army—ours or any other country's —soldiers going AWOL have been a problem, sometimes large, sometimes small. In World War II and the Korean War, it was a relatively insignificant worry, for the converse of the reasons it could be a problem currently. Today, with soldiers owning their own cars; with no taps, head counts, or reveille inspections to slow them down; and with no constant need for passes, a soldier is far freer to come and go than were his father and grandfather. A recent trend toward loosened discipline in schools and churches may also invite transgression on the part of young men unused to and unfamiliar with the structured life of a soldier.

Whatever the cause, the one sure way to reduce the problem (it can never be eliminated) is for platoon leaders, company commanders, and NCOs in the small unit chain to know their men, talk to them, find out what's bugging them (money, family problems, and women seem to lead the list), then help them to solve their problems. Simple interest in and sympathy with soldiers help many of them to stay on the straight and narrow.

To help solve soldiers' problems, NCOs and officers must know, among other things, how to get Red Cross help, how to find the Army Emergency Relief office, how Army Community Service can help families in trouble, where to call for emergency medical aid, where to find the Drug and Alcohol Abuse Center, how to contact Alcoholics Anonymous, and the telephone number of a duty chaplain after duty hours.

There are, of course, many other agencies that can help men and their families. These actions and activities are not simply to cut down AWOLs; that's the wrong reason for doing the right thing. The right reason is to help the troops and their families with problems that are real, serious, and sometimes unbelievably formidable and complex. Soldiers and their families get desperate; their problems can literally "make a grown man cry." A little understanding and compassion for the troops by the NCOs and junior officers and the judicious use of the three-day pass and emergency leave can go a long way toward keeping a soldier straight and helping him to avoid ruining his career.

Another way to help solve the AWOL problem is by close association with the police in the nearby community and a knowledge of the soldiers' off-post haunts. And into this picture enters the NCO. When he gets a call from the local sheriff or police that one of his men has been picked up drunk and disorderly and/or AWOL, the NCO has a great chance to find out about the man's problems while he is bringing him back to the post.

Difficulties have a way of compounding. A number of years ago, I was in the Airborne Department of the Artillery School at Fort Sill. One Sunday morning, I got a call from the local jail that the police were holding an NCO who wanted to see me. I dutifully went to the jail and found there, in a cell, a disheveled SFC who had worked for me previously in the G–1 section of the 82d Airborne Division. He was a marvelous soldier and NCO. But that morning, I found a confused, discouraged, dejected, broken soldier. His problem boiled down to a classic one: His wife left him so he went on a drunken AWOL spree. I bailed him out, took him back to the post, and listened for a long time to his tale of woe. I wrote a long, impassioned plea to the soldier's wife, telling her what a fine man her husband was and practically begging her to give him another chance. Unfortunately, I was not successful in saving the marriage, but I think that, because of my interest and willingness to help, I was able to save the sergeant.

Today, in some units, the AWOL problem seems to have abated. I asked a young major who had successfully commanded two companies in the 82d Airborne Division (his success is measured by the fact that he made major from below the zone) and who is now the XO of the 4/325th Parachute Infantry Battalion Combat Team in Italy (the only parachute outfit in Europe today) to comment on the AWOL problem and to tell me how he has handled the problem in his companies and in the 4/325th.

Here is what he had to say:

You could not have picked a less objective man to comment on AWOLs, I have never had much of a problem with them. The 4/325th currently has a negligible incidence of AWOLs. If a man makes a habit of AWOL, he will leave this battalion and the Army as well. Things are good today. We can be selective in our retention of soldiers. AWOLees, we can't use.

The primary reason for my lack of objectivity is that I can't suffer a man who would go AWOL. I have never encountered a good excuse from a man (I should be adding "or woman" lest I receive an EO complaint) who went AWOL. There are no good reasons. A soldier has too many sympathetic ears to which he can turn. The number of social organizations (or reasonable facsimiles) within the Army are legion. A person who goes AWOL should never again enjoy the absolute confidence of the chain of command or his peers. In a firefight, this man probably will not fire his weapon, or even worse, will run.

Even though there is a generation gap between me and the major I quote and even though we commanded company-sized units about thirty-five years apart, the answer to that problem still seems to be the same: Take care of the worthwhile soldiers and try to help them with their problems using all of the Army's and the local community's array of agencies. But if the soldier is incorrigible, or would be redeemed only at an inordinate cost of time and energy, get him out of the Army.

So it all boils down to this: Take care of your soldiers; they deserve it. (And believe me, they'll take care of you.)

The battalion is the best command job in the whole Army.

Battalion Command

There he stands: Alone, hands joined behind his back, chest up, stomach in, shoulders back, feet spread apart the width of his hips, fatigues well-fitted (well, they used to be before camouflaged fatigues and probably will be again), boots gleaming, green tabs worn proudly on his shoulder straps (which he has probably added to his fatigues just to display his green tabs), the mark of the commander. He surveys the scene with studied calm, experienced eye, and cool demeanor; he is the commander, the battalion commander, master of all he surveys, giving orders fearlessly and rapidly, whether on the drill field or in combat; his presence inspires the troops, calms the nervous, and shatters the foe—the enemy or the inspectors from higher headquarters. Or at least that is the way he might appear to the uninitiated.

Inwardly, the battalion commander is weighing, considering, analyzing a myriad of facts, out of the maze of which somehow he has to make a wise, just, rapid decision. But so be it. He still has the best job in the Army.

At the battalion level, for the first time in his career, the battalion commander has a staff that has the same elements and functions as the staffs of the most senior commander: personnel, intelligence, training and operations, and supply. Of course, he must also handle administration, maintenance, the mess, to say nothing of morale, welfare, and education. All of these functions fall to the lot of the battalion commander. And he loves it. This is the level at which it all comes together. This is the level for which the Army spends a great deal of time and money selecting the right officers; this is the level at which a unit gets its own number; this is the level, probably for the last time, at which a commander can get to know almost every one of his men by name and know a great deal about them and their problems, hopes, desires, and ambitions. This is the level at which the flow of regulations and policies generally stops; this is the level at which the commander knows how those policies and regulations work and is thus a font of information on the inner workings and hidden mechanisms of the Army as a whole. This is the level that the rest of the Army supports—if it is an infantry battalion—it is the level at which the superb commander can shine forth and make of his battalion a keenly tuned instrument of well-trained men and combat-ready materiel. It is also the level at which the incompetent or unlucky officer can break his pick.

The easily identifiable rewards to the successful commander are great: the War College, selection for colonel and perhaps eventual selection for general, key staff assignments, a brigade command. But the inner reward is greater: the knowledge that he could take a body of men, train them, live with them, fight with them, sorrow with them, lead them, cajole them, reward them, love them—and lead them successfully through mission after mission, in combat or in garrison.

And that's really why the battalion is the best command in the Army.

A committee is a group of the unfit appointed by the unwilling to do the unnecessary.

Boards, Councils, Committees, Special Assistants, and Other Crutches of Leadership

"The harder right instead of the easier wrong" is to make the chain of command work. It cannot work in the midst of an interlocking, entangling, helter-skelter, organization-boggling array of enlisted men's councils, junior officer councils, special assistants, boards, committees, and other ad hoc or continuous groups operating outside the normal structure. (If the normal structure can't hack it, change it—permanently.) Admittedly, there comes a time when an extraordinary task or mission requires the formation of a tailor-made task force. So be it. But disband it as soon as the mission is accomplished.

The organizations that do the most to inhibit the proper functioning of the chain of command are the EM councils that some well-intentioned commanders set up to advise them on their troop problems. In some units, each level of command has its own council, and some division commanders have handpicked enlisted men working full-time as their advisors.

What are the NCOs and young officers doing if such crutches are necessary to tell the CO at any level what his troops' problems are? What is the battalion sergeant major doing while some E-5 tells the CO the latest gossip from the division-level council? Why aren't the squad and section leaders not only listening to their troops (see Open-Door Policy) but trying to solve their problems? (I do hope that by now EM councils have been relegated to the slag heap of ill-conceived, uninspired, and devilishly destructive and infantile ideas.)

Another device used by some commanders, even at battalion level, to solve a slightly out-of-the-ordinary problem is to set up a special assistant to handle it. Then the special assistant with his newfound power, because he is acting directly for the boss, cuts across established staff lines, gets into the hair of the regular staff, gathers unto himself many functions, and causes tremendous confusion, disorganization, and waste. Special assistants should go the way of the vermiform appendix.

Committee meetings, in any organization, large or small, probably waste more time and people than any other management device. Committees are useful when they are small, limited, properly led, and made up of the people who have an interest in and knowledge of the subject. And the subject must be sharply defined and the leader ruthless in keeping the discussion on the subject if the committee is to do any good in a reasonable period of time. But committees are useless time-wasters when they are made up of vast numbers of disinterested folk who are present only because of some remote connection with the subject or because the committee organizer wanted to cover all possibilities. Worse still are committees made up of relatively high ranking individuals who bring along to meetings an array of backup action officers just in case a question on which they are supposed to be particularly knowledgeable might come up. The action officers wait interminable hours in anterooms "just in case."

As everyone knows, the camel is the result of a committee's efforts to design a horse. A committee by its very nature is unable to make a decision. It can gather facts, line up pros and cons, and list alternatives. For these purposes, a committee is sometimes useful. But only the man with the authority and the responsibility can make the final decision.

A military unit, with its staff and chain of command, is particularly well suited to handle almost any situation. Thus, anyone in a position of authority must scrutinize carefully and frequently the committees, boards, councils, and special assistants that subordinates may establish. He must analyze their *raisons d'être*, and if they are useless or only marginally useful, he must eliminate them. Only constant vigilance can prevent the organization chart from looking like the wiring diagram of an AM/FM stereo amplifier.

Look at the situation from a battalion commander's standpoint. He has a well-disciplined staff of officers and NCOs to administer, manage, and operate his battalion. He has no need to use special assistants or committees to analyze and solve problems. He is in a perfect position to handle his command without any resort to jerry-built structures.

Community Relations. U.S. Army photo

Remember the Golden Rule: Bosses are sometimes smart people.

Boss, Relations with

Any boss worth his job and money wants the truth. He wants to know what's going on. He wants the bad news as well as the good news. And generally speaking, he hates surprises sprung on him by *his* boss. He wants to think he knows everything going on in his organization before some outsider does. Here are a few rules for dealing with the boss.

1. Be honest and frank; a good boss will respect you for it.

2. Don't waffle the news; tell it like it is.

3. Give him the bad and the good; don't let him be surprised.

4. Make sure you have all the facts and, most importantly, both sides of the story (rarely is anything either as good or as bad as first reports indicate), but report, if necessary, with fragmentary news—if it is that important—properly identified as preliminary, unsubstantiated, first blush, as the case may be.

5. Don't kowtow, don't be brash; be yourself. Have confidence in yourself, do your homework, and you won't have to worry about what the boss thinks of you.

6. If you don't know the answer, say so; you might be embarrassed temporarily, but that's nothing compared to how you'll feel if you give an off-the-cuff, quick-reaction answer that the boss later learns is wrong and on which he may have made some decisions.

7. Don't exaggerate a boss's request; give him what he asks for —nothing more, nothing less. Be precise (but if you get a mission and can do it faster with fewer men, by all means do so).

8. Don't be a sycophant, the kind of minion who takes a boss's request, expands the requirement as he passes it on to action officers, and sets deadlines far in advance of what the boss actually wants or needs. He is the worst kind of self-server, because he piles additional work on his peers or his subordinates just because he

31

thinks it will make him personally look good to his boss. When he discovers his assistant's *modus operandi*, his boss should fire him forthwith. Unfortunately, a boss, like a wife, is often the last to find out.

Undoubtedly, I have been guilty of assigning to a boss's request a higher priority than he intended. Undoubtedly, I felt that I needed a little time to check out the answers. And I am just as certain that some of my subordinates have shortened deadlines or exploded the requirements of something I've asked for.

I remember one such occasion. I had just assumed a rather high ranking job on the Army staff. I mentioned to the executive officer (the job was sufficiently high ranking that it came equipped with a colonel as executive officer) that I was not happy with my desk (the chairman of the board of General Motors made do with something less pretentious) and wanted to look at some simpler ones. My intention was to go down into the bowels of the Pentagon and have one of the GSA types show me what he had in stock. Perhaps I did not make it clear to my XO that I was perfectly willing to go where the desks were. In any case, he had GSA, with some difficulty, deliver a desk to the hall outside my office so that I could inspect it there. I was embarrassed, chagrined, and more than somewhat unhappy with my XO's overreaction. This, coupled with a few other manifestations of Napoleonic tendencies on my XO's part, caused me to arrange his transfer to less demanding climes.

That honesty with one's boss is the best policy became abundantly clear to me during an incident that happened just as I had taken over command of a parachute artillery battery in New Guinea. The 11th Airborne Division, of which we were a part, was languishing on that torrid island, continuing our training and, I suppose, getting acclimated to the climate, the mosquitos, and the Australian bully beef, along with other canned and powdered delicacies that the quartermaster hoped, erroneously, we would think was food. We were not yet in combat and were living in pyramidal tents lined up along the taxiways of an abandoned airfield. In my battery, there was what the troops referred to loathsomely as a "barracks thief." In the open living necessitated by pyramidal tents with flaps up, the thief had an easy time indulging his lightfingered habits. He also had ridden the sick book so frequently under the previous commander that he could arrange to be in the tent area while most of the battery was out on a training mission.

Finally, shortly after I assumed command of the battery, this splendid chap was caught red-handed. The senior NCOs, without my knowledge, arranged a "kangaroo court" during which the culprit was tried, convicted, and punished—summarily. The sentence was executed by a few of the tougher troops, who took the convicted thief to a stream bed in a jungle area behind the battery street and literally used him for a punching bag. At the completion of the punishment, the NCOs reported to my XO the whereabouts of the victim, stating that he was in need of medical treatment. In due time, the XO had the man delivered to the hospital.

The next day, I received a call from a very irate hospital commander, who berated me for the kind of officer I was, the kind of soldiers I had, and the kind of treatment they had leveled upon the victim. The hospital commander was undoubtedly an inspiration for a character in M*A*S*H*, so scornful was he of the regular side of the Army. Nevertheless, I took my lumps in silence and ended the conversation with a less than eloquent "Yes, sir."

I reported the incident to my battalion commander who, in turn, reported to the division artillery commander. Shortly thereafter, I received a call from the DivArty CG. With some fear and trepidation—after all, young captains are not often favored with a call from a brigadier general—I took the phone. The DivArty CG asked me if what he had heard about the incident was true. I admitted that "yes, sir, there had been a kangaroo court, that yes, sir, the man had been found guilty, and, yes, sir, the NCOs had beaten the hell out of the victim." The CG then said: "Well, Captain, that's the sort of thing that should reduce the thievery around your battery, shouldn't it?" My "yes, sir" again ended a very embarrassing conversation. Fortunately, that was the last I heard of the incident. The victim never returned to duty with the 11th Airborne Division, I suspect he never stole from his fellow soldiers again, and indeed thievery did abate, not only in my battery, but in other units of the division as the story spread. I do not advocate this sort of justice; I simply report that that's what happened.

Years later, I commanded the 3d Armored Div Arty in Hanau, Germany. One of the assistant division commanders was also stationed there and had an office directly below mine in Hutier Kaserne. He and I often played squash at lunchtime. One day, however, I had a match with another player and came back to the office about 1330. The ADC called for me and, after I reported to him, said rather irascibly, "Where the hell have you been? After all, it's one-thirty." I replied almost equally heatedly: "You know perfectly well where I've been—I've been playing squash." That ended the incident; I had disarmed the ADC. (But be careful, you have to know the players.) That ADC gave me, incidentally, one of the finest OER's in my file. And he never did beat me at squash.

To sum up and state simply: Do unto your boss as you would have your subordinates do unto you.

In brief, be brief.

Briefings

These days, briefings have long since lost their original function: to give a busy man a short, concise, complete report either for his information or from which he can make a decision. A briefing today may be anywhere from five minutes to five hours.

The best briefers are those who *(a)* know their subject, *(b)* organize their material logically, *(c)* present their matter in understandable, clear English (not in their mother tongue—R & D, Comptroller, Finance, AG, or other disciplines that have a language all their own as foreign as Amharic to everyone except an insider or an Ethiopian), and *(d)* key their briefings to the briefee's knowledge of the subject.

A briefing must follow a logical pattern. One sequence might be as follows:

1. Purpose (decision or information)
2. Precise statement of problem or subject
3. General outline of the briefing ("Here's what I am going to cover")
   a. Background (only enough facts to bring the briefee up to date)
   b. Pertinent facts
   c. Problems
   d. Courses of action and pros and cons of each
   e. Summary
4. The briefing itself according to the outline above
5. Recommendation (clear, precise, couched in such terms that the boss need say only "approved" or "disapproved")

A good briefer uses simple, understandable charts to get his points across. The charts need not have been made by a commercial artist; clarity is far more important than artistic merit. (One punctilious four-star general for whom I worked as SGS was perfectly content with butcher paper charts *provided* they were clear and readable). If the charts are easily understandable, don't read them. Simply give the briefee time to read them. A good briefer follows the eyes of the briefee and knows when to move to the next chart — a nod of the head or a look at the briefer will usually tell him when to move on.

If the chart is somewhat complex, walk over to it and explain what's on it. Speak to the briefee—not the chart. Use a pointer in your hand closest to the chart. Don't turn your back on the briefee. A really superb briefer does not *read* his briefing. He speaks from his charts and an outline. This requires intimate knowledge of his subject, which is, of course, a prerequisite for being a briefer on that particular subject in the first place. The major hazard of speaking from charts instead of reading the briefing is one of timing. The briefing that is read can be timed precisely, whereas the "spoken" (as opposed to read) briefing can consume far more time than planned if the briefer does not stick precisely to his outline. But again, the good briefer can keep his eye on the clock and cover his important points in the allocated time.

The old saw about the southern preacher who gave good sermons is equally applicable to a briefing. Asked about how he was able to give such good, easily understood, and memorable sermons, the preacher said simply, "I tell 'em what I'm going to tell 'em, then I tell 'em, then I tell 'em what I told 'em." In our parlance, that means one of your first charts is the outline of what you're going to cover, then the next series of charts explains your subject matter, and your final chart sums up the presentation.

As a major on the division staff of the 11th Airborne, I learned the hard way some of the basics of giving a briefing. We were on Okinawa ready to move to occupy Japan just before the end of World War II. We had flown to Okinawa in great haste and on short notice from Luzon and were preparing to fly on to Atsugi. (We would be the first division to land in Japan.) I was the Division Air Officer in the G-3 section. The CG called for a briefing on the details of the move to Atsugi. Naturally, it fell to my lot to give the presentation. Rather confidently, I went to the CG's tent to discuss (rather than brief) the situation with him. After about thirty seconds he said to me: "Don't you have any charts? How am I supposed to know what the hell you're talking about if I can't see it? Why can't I find some staff officers who know what they are talking about," etc. etc. After that session, my performance as a staff officer exploded geometrically. The next day I was better prepared.

As one moves up the line in the Army, briefings tend to get more complex. I always initiated a briefer with the Flanagan rule: Make it simple; if I can understand it, anyone can.

Gen. Ben Harrell, when he was a senior staff officer on the Army Staff, put it another way. He served notice thusly on a briefer of a particularly complex subject at the beginning of the briefing: "Colonel, we're not leaving here until I understand this stuff."

We in the military are called upon to brief not only our own superiors but many other visitors and dignitaries. One of those I enjoyed most was the one I presented to Prince Charles of England. He visited the Presidio of San Francisco and came to my office for the briefing. I gave him about fifteen minutes on the U.S. Army at home and abroad. And even though it was at 0800 on a Saturday morning, Prince Charles seemed to pay close attention. I suspect that he hardly heard a word, but he has so trained himself that he gave every evidence of rapt concentration. He also has a splendid sense of humor. After I escorted him outside my office, he walked over to a group of people who were standing in line in a roped-off area. He went down the line shaking hands and greeting the spectators. He came back to me and whispered: "I'm running for office." And, I said: "Sir, I think you've already been elected."

Another briefing that I relished was one I gave to a visiting Russian major general. These days, Russians, especially Russian generals, are usually caricatured as beetle-browed, dour, scowling, steely-eyed, menacing, stolid, or distrustful—or all of the above.

But Russians do have a sense of humor. In the days before the recent invasion and smothering of Afghanistan by the "invited" hordes of Russian military, a Soviet major general and a small entourage visited San Francisco. As is the custom when ranking military officers and other distinguished visitors come to the City by the Bay, the protocol people who arrange these things called upon the Sixth Army commander to host a visit by the Soviet general.

And so the itinerary was arranged: briefing at Sixth Army head-quarters, tour of the Presidio, cocktails at the CG's quarters, and dinner at the officers' club. At my headquarters, I personally briefed the visiting general with very carefully unclassified remarks and charts.

Later, during the cocktail session at my quarters, the atmosphere thawed. Suitable gifts were exchanged (the Russian general proudly and with some fanfare presented me with a model of the latest Soviet tank).

Then, with tongue in cheek, I said to the Soviet general through his interpreter, "General, I want you to know that everything I told you this afternoon at the briefing was classified Secret and should be treated as such."

The Soviet general, not to be outdone, promptly replied, "And I want you to know, General, that the briefing will remain a secret between your Army and mine."

One final point, and one of the most important I can make about briefings: A commander at any level should give his own briefings and not rely on a staff officer to do it for him. The most effective briefings for one's superiors is one in which you, the junior commander, invite the visiting senior to your office or conference room and then brief him using charts, slides, or graphs. The commander thus puts himself—not a staff officer—on the line and on the spot. If you're on top of your command, you have nothing to fear; if you don't know the details of an answer, don't bluff. Tell the briefee what you know and then tell him you will forward the details by letter or phone.

Carefully prepared briefings at battalion and company level are just as important as at any higher level. This is especially true of company and battalion commanders briefing their seniors. The outline I have given applies at lower levels just as well as it does in the Pentagon (where a lot of briefers, of course, are lieutenant colonels and majors). At the lower levels, the various steps may be shorter; some may be eliminated. But the logical sequence and knowledge of your subject are the important things; trust yourself —it will pay great rewards.

Give a man a job and let him do it.

Centralization and the Evils Thereof

The greatest impetus to overcentralization has undoubtedly been the proliferation of and improvement in communications. Pigeons, signal flags, smoke, and horse-mounted couriers have long since given way to telephones, radios, teletypes, and television, which handle a phenomenal volume of words rapidly, secretly, and accurately. Thus, reports of actions of platoons in combat can easily be flashed to the highest level of government within the hour (witness the communications for the ill-fated raid to free the hostages in Iran, wherein the President of the United States had direct communications with the raid commander in the desert); minor operations can be planned, watched, and quarterbacked from the major commander's operations center; almost anyone can talk to anyone else over secure telephone lines at any hour of night or day.

And with this proliferation of communications, there is the concomitant desire of everyone up the line to know exactly what everyone else down the line is doing. (During the Vietnam War, President Johnson received detailed daily briefings on the combat situation.) Hence, in the past few decades, we've seen decision making move swiftly up the chain, we've been burdened with vastly increased requirements for reports of all kinds to support the decision makers, and we've been traumatized at lower levels by more and more centralization.

But that's wrong. That violates the basic precept of giving a man a job, giving him the resources with which to accomplish it, and then letting him do it. To follow that time-honored, field-tested principle, one must trust his subordinates, one must expect mistakes and failure from the young and inexperienced, one must be

40

content to wait a little longer, and one must have, in the words of a wise and mature commander, "patience and perseverance."

To decentralize is not to divest oneself of all responsibility. On the contrary, he who decentralizes must also continue to check on mission accomplishment, but in a methodical, planned way—not the nit-picking, meddling, frantic checking done by nervous and insecure bosses. A wise leader gives a man a job and a deadline, if necessary, and then, after a reasonable time, checks to see how he's doing. A young leader may need guidance and advice; an older one may need a quick karate chop for emphasis; but all subordinates need to be looked in on for three reasons: *(a)* to demonstrate interest on the senior's part, *(b)* to see how things are coming, and *(c)* to give the subordinate a chance to show off his progress and good work.

Nonetheless, those good principles have a way of breaking up on the rocky road to success. When success means everything, when men demand credit for themselves, these principles take second priority. (General Abrams used to quote General of the Army George C. Marshall, who said: "There's no limit to the amount of good a man can do if he doesn't care who gets the credit.")

Not only does centralization take over in a success-oriented environment, but so does stovepiping, that insidious management tool by which functional areas are lined up vertically and operated from the top. This system takes out of the hands of the subordinate commander responsibility for functions that he formerly had. Thus, communications in the field are directed by a headquarters in the United States; hospitals are managed by a central headquarters in Texas; NCO promotions are all made in Washington; and even, as mind-boggling a thought as it is, a three-star Army CG does not command the post on which his headquarters is located; that's done from FORSCOM. The subordinate may even still have the moral or real responsibility for a function, but no longer, under stovepiping, does he have the authority or the clout to influence the action. There are probably some legitimate and valuable stovepipe arrangements abroad in the land (the automated pay of the Army from Fort Ben Harrison, for example), but they are exceptions.

Consider the Lewis and Clark expedition as a case study of decentralization. That expedition is one of the greatest illustrations of the theory of giving men a job and letting them do it. President Jefferson simply said to two young captains, Lewis and Clark (this is not a direct quote; fortunately, President Jefferson had no hidden mikes to record his words for posterity): "Get an expedition together; go off and explore the Louisiana Purchase territories, and report back what you find." Eighty-five hundred miles and many months later, they did just that. Two young captains!

Today, for such a mission, there would be, first, a huge, bloated planning staff in Washington with major generals as heads of each staff agency; there would probably be a four-star in charge in the field; all kinds of civilian special assistants would advise on Indian affairs, geography, minerals, climate, weather, routes, and so forth, with each ungovernable and independent civilian reporting directly back to his boss in whatever agency of government he came from; there would be environmental impact studies, equal opportunity agencies (are the Indians getting the shaft?), economic surveys, affirmative action requirements, and voluminous records and reports; there would be redundant means of communication; a gargantuan supply tail; and an accompanying press corps writing endless copy about the troops' living conditions, senior officers' perks, and the millions of dollars of taxpayers' money being spent. Brilliant TV commentators would second-guess every decision, and the cameras would zoom in on Indian tepees, ditched wagons, and faulty saddles.

Consider these real-life examples of centralization: To remove a set of government quarters from the housing list of a post, an assistant secretary of the Army had to give permission; an Army headquarters civilian safety officer directed that the swimming pools at Fort Riley, which I commanded, close at a certain hour because of light conditions (presumably, I was incapable of making such a brilliant judgment); finally, the message directing implementation of an automated system for Army commissaries contained this forgettable line: "If an exemption is justifiable (e.g., extremely low line item volume) such exemption must be requested, through channels, from HQ Department of the Army accompanied by a complete justification for the request." By which time the overstocked and unwanted item would be outdated, rotted, and cluttering up the storeroom.

The preceding examples of centralization are obviously broad and seemingly above the level of interest of battalion commanders and their subordinates down the chain. Nonetheless, the principles remain valid and applicable no matter what the level.

A commander who understood the principle of giving a man a job to do and then letting him do it (which is the heart of decentralization) was one of the great division commanders of World War II, Gen. Joseph M. Swing, who commanded the 11th Airborne from its activation in February 1943 through its training in North Carolina, Louisiana, and New Guinea, through combat on Leyte and Luzon, through the occupation of Japan. He left the division in the summer of 1948 from Sapporo, Hokkaido, Japan, to become a corps commander. One incident in particular illustrates General Swing's willingness to trust a subordinate with a relatively large task—large at least in the eyes and mind of a young officer on the division staff.

Toward the end of World War II, I was a twenty-three-year-old major, two and a half years out of West Point. (For WW II days, that was only a little better than par for the course—there were twenty-four-year-old battalion commanders, twenty-seven-year-old regimental commanders, and a thirty-seven-year-old division commander, Maj. Gen. James M. Gavin, CG of the 82nd Airborne Division in combat in Europe.) By early August 1945, the 11th Airborne Division had been withdrawn from combat and was in bivouac in various locations south of Manila and around Lipa, Luzon. The division, like many other units that had defeated the Japanese on Luzon, was awaiting the implementation of Olympic and Coronet, the operations by which General MacArthur would assemble and deploy vast forces to invade the home islands of Japan.

But then it happened—on August 6, 1945, the nuclear age became a reality—the United States dropped the first atomic bomb on an enemy target, Hiroshima. A few days later, with the dropping of the second atomic bomb on Nagasaki, the short-lived era of actual nuclear war was over. Shortly thereafter, the Japanese sued for peace. Operations Olympic and Coronet became "what might have been," and the need immediately arose for forces to move swiftly to Japan to occupy the home islands. Because the 11th Airborne was lightly equipped and very air-mobile (although during the war it had been assigned the same arduous and prolonged missions as the heavier and more powerfully equipped standard infantry divisions), it was selected to move by air, first to Okinawa and then to Japan, to spearhead the occupation.

Sixth Army, the parent headquarters under which the 11th served, had alerted the division to be prepared to move out on forty-eight hours' notice. At 0530, on Saturday morning, August 11, 1945, Sixth Army implemented that alert. We had forty-eight hours. General Swing immediately sent me, the G-3 Air, to Sixth Army Headquarters to follow up on the alert. There, at about 0900 that day, the Sixth Army staff planner told me that at that very moment aircraft were on their way to Lipa airfield to start to move the 11th to Okinawa. The forty-eight hour cushion had evaporated; we now had four. I immediately notified the division and returned to the headquarters. I reported to General Swing (the G-3 was ill and out of action). I can't remember General Swing's exact words, but in effect he told me to get going and move the division.

We had four airfields available to us: Lipa, Nichols, Nielson, and Clark. I sent a captain liaison officer to each field and then worked directly with the regimental commanders to alert them and to tell them to which field to take their troops; I coordinated with the G-4 to send the necessary trucks to move the troops and then informed my liaison officers of the number of troops and the arrival times at their respective fields. We had no advance notice of the number or types of aircraft the U.S. Army Air Corps had rounded up to move us. But round them up they did. We used C-46s, B-24s with about fourteen men crammed into the bomb bays, and whatever C-54s the Air Corps could muster on such short notice. (By the time we moved from Okinawa to lead the forces into Japan for its occupation, the Air Corps had assembled from all over the world all available C-54s. Knowing the type of aircraft made planning a great deal easier.) As the aircraft arrived at each field, we loaded them with the troops, which had arrived there only shortly before. Finally, by Monday night (and my liaison officers and I had not taken even a nap since Saturday morning), we had the bulk of the division on Okinawa ready to move on to Japan. The frustrating arrival of the monsoons almost coincidentally with our arrival on Okinawa and the continuing kamikaze attacks is yet another story.

The point is this: General Swing gave me a mission, freedom to deal with the necessary staff and commanders, the wherewithal to do the job, and then a free hand to accomplish my mission—move the 11th Airborne to Japan. Naturally, I kept him and the Chief of Staff informed of what was going on. But I felt a tremendous responsibility and consequently worked to the limit to accomplish my job. Reward? Great satisfaction plus a steak dinner (the meat was very tough as I recall—must have been carabao) in the general's mess with my four liaison officers on Monday night after we had the division almost completely closed on Okinawa.

What's the message for a battalion, company, or even a platoon commander? Stop meddling; let the chain work; get out of the hair of someone who is trying to do a job. Have faith.

Ceremonies

Part and parcel of the military tradition is ceremonies. Like any-thing else, they too can be overdone. But a military formation, thoroughly planned and precisely executed by well-trained troops, is a mark of pride and esprit for units participating therein. Granted there is no longer a need to fire a cannon at or around sundown (the forerunner of our retreat ceremony), which used to be necessary to recall the troops to the fort when the day's work outside the fort was done. But there is tradition in almost every walk of life of any substance. For better or worse, the military probably has more traditions than any other institution.

A military ceremony is worse than useless if it is not done with pride, style, precision, and military polish. Honor guards, particu-larly, have been prostituted and desecrated over the years. In an attempt at individualism, many units have introduced gimmicks and uniform aberrations that lend a circus (or worse) air to the honor guard proceedings. Gimmickry is no substitute for soldierly precision.

Often, our parades and reviews are barely controlled mob scenes. For example, consider a present-day battalion review or parade. The companies line up in company fronts. When the time comes for the units to march off the field, the commander of the troops commands: "Pass in review." The company commander on the right of the line gives the command: "Column right, march." Thereupon, the company, even the most military and best drilled, makes a right turn during which the unit seems to disintegrate as viewed from the reviewing stand. The left side of the company speeds around the turn trying to get back in line, and it is not until the company does two more columns left and starts passing in front of the reviewing stand that there is any semblance of order, straight lines, and proper cadence.

46

One enterprising commander (in all modesty I must admit that he was I—and the following drill is probably one I picked up from someone else) developed a drill that bests the present system for precision and soldierliness. At a battalion review, for example, I required that the companies be organized into platoons (as if this were any great news) of three squads. There can be three or four depending on the company, troop, or battery size. Thus, as the companies face the reviewing stand, the companies are lined up with the platoons and squads in depth. Each platoon, of course, is three men wide and each company nine or twelve men wide—depending upon the number of its platoons. At any rate, at the command "Pass in review," the company commander on the right of the line gives the command: "Company, right face." Then the first platoon commander gives the command: "First platoon, forward march." At successive intervals, each platoon commander in the battalion gives his platoon a similar command.

Now back to the first platoon leader. He is on the left flank of the platoon which is in a platoon front. At the first turn, he commands: "By the left flank, march." At the next turn, again: "By the left flank, march." At this point, he moves to the front and center of his platoon which is again in a platoon front ready to pass in review. And behind that platoon, in succeeding ranks of platoons, in platoon fronts, is the rest of the battalion.

This kind of formation, adaptable at company, battalion, and brigade ceremonies, offers these advantages: *(a)* Each platoon leader is out in front of his platoon and he is actually leading and commanding it; *(b)* each man in the platoon is more visible and thus more important; *(c)* it is far more military than the formations dictated by the current manuals; *(d)* it is very simple but precise; and *(e)* it introduces no commands or maneuvers with which the troops are not familiar.

Let's face it: Military formations have long since lost their utilitarian need in combat—to move troops to the proper line or to deploy them rapidly to permit them to fire their muskets or launch their arrows at the enemy only ten yards away. Those were the tactics of the battlefields in the days of Gustavus II and the Thirty Years' War (Right front into line! Squads right! etc.). But such tactics will not, in themselves, save the lives of American soldiers on some distant and unknown battlefield of the future.

Why then do we need ceremonies? Why this anachronism?

Ceremonies, parades, honor guards, and reviews, and marches (if they are not overdone) do this: They preserve a tradition—and many a Medal of Honor and Victoria Cross has been won by a man who has been upholding the tradition or the honor of his unit; they make a unit cohesive and competitive; they provide ready and simple ways of moving troops from one point to another; they provide a military and traditional formation at which deserving soldiers can be given awards in front of their units and officers and men can be retired with dignity and distinction; and perhaps, most importantly, they make soldiers look, act, and think like soldiers.

Frocking of Col. John T. Quinn. U.S. Army photo

Use it; it's the only way that we can run this Army properly.

Chain of Command

Throughout our careers, we have been taught to use the chain of command, to make each leader at each level responsible for what his unit does or fails to do. Yet, too often (see Centralization), we have violated this precept. This is a serious error.

First, the leaders in the chain of command are commanders. They have responsibilities. But for every violation of the chain, for every bit of authority chipped away, for every committee that operates out of the chain, for every special assistant, there is a diminution of that responsibility. After a certain amount of it, the commander's frustration gives way to cynicism and disinterest and he says: "To hell with it; if that's the way they're going to run this outfit, I'm not going to give a damn. Let those smart-ass staff officers up the line do the worrying."

Second, the chain can get the job done if utilized properly. That's what it's for. Not even Napoleon could command ten thousand men individually—and part of the reason for his downfall was that he tried to do just that. Even he had to have a chain of subordinates, each in charge of successively smaller units, to pass the commands down the line.

Third, if we are going to make commanders responsible, we must give them the authority that goes with it.

Fourth, and probably foremost, it permits the commander, whether at field Army or platoon level, to issue orders and to know that the chain will see to it that all men comply. (But only to the degree that the chain works.)

One simple illustration of the chain of command in action: On REFORGER III (an acronym for Return of Forces to Germany), the First Division troops (minus one brigade) from Fort Riley, 11,056 men, arrived in Europe in battle dress but with desert colors

49

(browns and tans) of their helmet camouflage covers showing. Obviously, in the fall in the forests of Germany, desert colors were inappropriate. The 7th Corps commander duly noted this discrepancy and mentioned it causally to the by-then red-faced division commander (me). That evening, at the brigade commanders and division staff meeting, I directed that each of the 11,056 men turn his camouflage cover over to the green side by 0700 the next morning. The chain of command worked; by the 0700 formation the next morning, not a brown and tan camouflage cover was in evidence. A committee system could hardly have accomplished that mission. And the EM councils and junior officer councils might still be debating the wisdom and value of the order.

The principle is as applicable at the battalion and even lower levels as it is at higher levels. The battalion and company commanders know many if not all of their men and have a tendency to bypass the chain to give an order, make a correction, assign a mission. Obviously, the part of the chain that is bypassed has no idea of what has happened—a situation often leading to disaster. So stifle the direct approach to running a unit; keep the chain intact; and if in some sort of an emergency one must end-run the chain, inform the bypassed part at the earliest moment.

The chain of command can also be formed of very few links. For part of the time I commanded the 674th Parachute FA Battalion, we were stationed at Camp Wood, outside Kumamoto, Japan. Because I was the senior of the lieutenant colonels commanding the two airborne battalions there, occasionally I acted as post commander in his absence. (For a long time, he was a non-airborne type; we probably drove him to drink and extended leaves.)

During one such interval, I decided that, as the commander of the 674th, I wanted the post to change some regulation or other. The significance was so minimal that today I cannot remember what it was. At any rate, I had the request duly prepared, I signed it recommending approval, and sent it up to post. Then I moved there as acting Post CO. Among other papers, the post adjutant brought in the request I had initiated at the 674th. From my new vantage point, I saw the situation in a different light (as I knew I would) and thereupon disapproved the request and, over my signature, sent it back to the CO of the 674th with a few paragraphs of explanation, none of which praised him for his astuteness or common sense.

My fondest hope is that someplace in the musty and extensive archives of the U.S. Army that piece of correspondence has assumed its rightful place as an example of brevity, expediency, and perplexity in the chain of command. I can only hope that in the future, some eager, liberal archivist will find that piece of correspondence, wonder at its significance, and then write a lengthy tome on the subject of "Enigmas Extracted While Studying the Organization of the Army Circa 1953 and the Insanity and/or Bewilderment of the Then Extant Battalion-Post Commanders."

Ah, well, the chain worked. Be sure to use it.

Ultimate committee, Joint Chiefs of Staff and unit specified commanders, July 12, 1983, Pentagon. DoD photo by R. D. Ward

Keep the troops informed.

Commander's Comments

Whether it's at morning parade (which see), in the daily bulletin, or in the post newspaper, the commander at every level has the obligation to tell the troops "what's going on." This obligation does not in any sense mean that the commander must hold a rap session with his subordinates to decide what to do; quite the contrary. Once a commander has made his decision (and to help him make that decision he certainly uses his staff and subordinates to the utmost), he announces it with as much explanation as needed. This may be short or long depending (to use an old military cliché) on the situation.

Many commanders with a post or a unit newspaper, or even a battalion weekly handout, write a column or an item for each issue of the paper. To be successful—that is, read—the items must be timely, short, important, and written in a style the troops will understand. (They need not be ungrammatical; they need only be understandable.) The topics for the commander's comments might run the gamut from field training dates and other training matters, to AWOLs, safety, the GED program, the Red Cross, and education opportunities. Obviously, there is a vast array of subjects the commander needs to discuss (*tell* is a better word here—there's going to be little direct discussion) with the troops, subjects that are hard to get out through the chain or that need not get out through the chain. A commander's column is not a major violation of the chain of command. It is simply a chance for the commander to express his views on a variety of subjects that he would not be able to comment on otherwise.

Columns of this sort are read also by the wives of the troops and the officers. Occasionally, it's wise to address them, specifically to help explain policies or procedures in which they have a vital interest (field training dates, off-post operations, officer and NCO arrivals, Army Community Service activities, etc.).

U.S. soldiers are intelligent. They react and respond in direct proportion to what they know and believe. Thus, the prudent commander tells his troops as much as he is able about the situation, day-to-day problems, policies from higher levels, his own policies, and his decisions. And he must be accurate; there is nothing harder than trying to call back and squelch an erroneous piece of information.

A well-informed soldier is a far better soldier than one who is disgruntled, questioning, and feeds on rumors, half-truths, and ambiguities. And it's at the battalion and company level where all this troop information comes to focus. How battalion, company, and platoon leaders handle this problem determines the well-being, morale, and esprit of the whole Army. After all, the Army, in the final analysis, is made up simply of x number of platoons.

Two people are rarely on exactly the same wave length.

Communications

At Camp Mackall, North Carolina, the original home and basic training ground for the 11th Airborne Division during World War II, our last crusade, a group of cadre men presented a demonstration to some neophyte soldiers (myself—a brand-new second lieutenant—included) that vividly illustrated the difficulty of orally passing an uncomplicated order from one man to another accurately. The demonstration was simplicity itself and designed to show only how the spoken word can get garbled in transmission— even when there are no radios involved. In the demonstration, the instructor called to the platform ten men from the audience—at random. He spaced them around the stage at about three-pace intervals. Then he read in a whisper a short ten- or twelve-word order to the first man and told him to pass it on exactly as he had heard it to the next man and so on down the line. Finally, the instructor asked the last man to write down the message exactly as he received it from the man next to him. The instructor then compared that message to the one he had given the first man. It bore no resemblance and was completely garbled. Thus was demonstrated the difficulty of communication by the spoken word. (Try this test someday in your own outfit.)

As if relaying a message accurately were not a sufficient problem unto itself, consider some of the problems of the written word, the convoluted writing, twisted phrases, and stilted verbiage that pass for English prose these days.

"At this point in time," and "at that point in time," were made popular during the Watergate hearings. But those phrases simply mean "now" and "then."

Another gem is a direct quote from a magazine article. The

writer wanted to "transfuse the perspective of higher management to enhance the judgment of the decision makers at lower levels of management." Presumably he wanted the boss to talk to his subordinates.

Throughout the daily flow of messages, papers, letters, and cables in almost any profession, there is a steady stream of stilted, obtuse, pontifical, pedantic language that boggles the mind. In the Army, we have adopted stuffy euphemisms for many time-honored and once easily understood terms: a mess hall is now a dining facility; a gym is a physical fitness facility; a laundry is a fabricare center; barracks are living facilities; a mess sergeant is a dining facility manager; a KP is a dining room attendant (if there is still such a person); a kitchen is a food preparation facility. We don't "pay" troops any more, we "effect their payment"; we don't "spend" money, we "outlay" it; we don't "try again," we "embark upon a second iteration"—the list goes on and on.

In addition to euphemisms and other mealy-mouthed circumlocutions, one of the greatest deterrents to clarity of the written or oral word is the use of the passive voice. The passive voice is definitely the voice to use if you do not care to identify the subject, if you wish to be obscure, and if you are trying to muddy the waters. (Diplomats undoubtedly use the passive voice deliberately on many occasions; so do politicians.)

But if you want clarity, brevity, and understanding, use the active voice. This simply means that each sentence has a subject, a predicate, and an object. It means that you can tell clearly who did what to whom. In military orders, it means that you know which unit is supposed to do exactly what.

One commander in Europe was so insistent on the use of the active voice that he directed his adjutant general to set up classes on the subject for all the staff officers in the headquarters. Rarely thereafter did a cable, message, paper, or letter with even a hint of the passive voice obfuscating the prose darken the commander's desk. It saved him from apoplexy and the author from oral or written abuse. (I was that CINCUSAREUR's Secretary of the General Staff; I made a number of points with action officers by changing their passive verbs to active verbs before they got to the CINC.)

There is another side to the matter of communications. It's probably a rewrite of the golden rule "Silence is golden." This is applicable to any soldier or officer, particularly if he doesn't know what he is talking about. Senior commanders have a tendency to believe what officers and soldiers in the field tell them. This is great and admirable, for it shows that the commander is getting out and seeing for himself what the situation is in his command. But many times, some young lieutenant or sergeant (or general) will sound off about something that, though true in his case, is peculiar only to his unit, or he may give only one side of the story or exaggerate grossly. Yet the "old man" (and that includes company and battalion commanders) thinks that the situation is abominable, widespread, or both. He comes roaring back to his headquarters breathing fire and looking for the dumb staff officer who allowed such a deplorable situation to develop. Thereafter, staff officers and/or unit commanders spend many hours sometimes needlessly explaining away a problem that never existed or existed only in isolation.

This does not mean that subordinates should not be frank and open with the boss—quite the opposite: It means that when you are frank and open, you must also be correct and complete.

There is something of a corollary to this principle. We all know that when a general says something, the result is a lot of motion—up, down, and sideways. Someone has to write a paper, or a unit has to do something it had not intended to do. Thus, generals must guard very carefully against making unnecessary suggestions, or expressing opinions no matter how offhandedly. General Abrams, making one of his more quotable and important utterances, said: "Generals should never miss the opportunity to remain silent." And privates, corporals, and lieutenants may also hope that colonels and lieutenant colonels never miss the opportunity to remain silent.

One might even long wistfully and nostalgically for those never-to-return days when messages were sent by semaphore or Morse code; the messages were concise and precise, and the chain of command *had* to work because that was the most certain way to get a message to all the troops. And it kept the very high commanders out of the hair of their subordinates.

Communications are at best difficult. (Even a simple yes or no

can be misinterpreted.) Yet we tend to make language far more difficult with pomposity (which some writers and speakers confuse
with erudition), euphemisms, and the passive, inexact voice. Precision is what we need; dictionaries and grammars are cheap.

*Don't forget: it's the Great American Public,
the G.A.P., who pay the taxes.*

Community Relations

Near Army installations, there are communities, some large, some small, that to varying degrees support the Army post with housing, shopping facilities, entertainment of all sorts (some good, some bad), theaters, and restaurants. We in the military profession must get along with the people of these towns and cities.

Admittedly, the towns near Army posts derive a great deal of benefit from the Army: jobs, industry, wives (and these days, husbands), and the soldier's dollar. Some communities are far more dependent on the post they abut than others. Nonetheless, post-community relations are a two-way affair, and each side, the military and civilian, must contribute to the harmony.

There are any number of ways to enhance this accord, and these steps are not limited to the senior commander and his staff; company and battalion commanders can practice them just as profitably. Here are some of them:

1. Have officers and the NCOs join the local fraternal organizations and attend their luncheons, dinners, and ceremonies.

2. Invite the civic leaders to post activities; this includes battalion field days and even company and battery parties occasionally.

3. Check with the local leaders whenever a commander is about to make a decision that might have an impact on the community.

4. Permit troops and units to assist in community projects (church repairs, baseball diamond leveling, stream clearance), provided that the projects are sanctioned by Army Regulations and don't bring the wrath of labor unions down on your head.

5. Put on demonstrations (skydiving, parades, firepower, field days, etc.) to which the whole community is invited.

6. Establish a post-community council to discuss mutual prob-

lems (racial tension, drug sales, discrimination of any sort). This is one council that does not violate the chain of command.

7. Set up, on holidays, an open house with displays of military equipment, skydiving, personnel carrier rides, tank demonstrations, parades, and so on. The list is limited only by imagination. And they can be done at very little cost.

8. Have an open line between the commander or his chief of staff and the local mayor or city manager to handle rapidly any serious problems that might arise. (The open line is real, telephone, and implied, close rapport and understanding.)

9. Establish close liaison between the provost marshal and the chief of police to enforce such regulations as uniforms in town and to include perhaps joint patrols on payday weekends near known trouble spots. Battalion commanders should certainly follow this step.

10. Set up joint golf, tennis, softball, and other sports tournaments with the local citizenry.

11. Encourage the local merchants to support the activities of the local chapter of AUSA.

12. Cooperate on fund-raising projects that are mutually beneficial.

13. Adopt an orphanage or similar activity; a whole battalion could get involved in this one.

When I was commanding the 674th Airborne Field Artillery Battalion at Camp Wood, Japan, after our return from Korea in 1953, the local civilian Catholic priest, a missionary who said Mass for us on Sundays, asked me to assist him in setting up a Boys' Town for the orphans of Kumamoto, the city near Camp Wood. I discussed the project with my officers and senior NCOs, and we decided that it was an eminently worthy task. We gave the project widespread publicity on our two-battalion post, but the troops of the 674th took it as their personal goal to set up a Boys' Town. We collected donations sufficient for the fathers to buy some acreage and buildings near our drop zone. (Some very zealous NCOs even took a drag from each payday poker game to donate to Boys' Town.) The troops pitched in to work during their off-duty time. Ultimately, there was indeed a Boys' Town, thanks to the 674th. The Japanese were so impressed and grateful for the orphanage that they made a movie of the whole project for showing throughout Japan. (Fortunately, they did not name it Colonel Flanagan's Boys' Town; Spencer Tracy wouldn't have liked that.)

Long gone are the days when a post commander, unhappy with the actions of a nearby community, can vent his wrath by placing the whole town or city "off limits" to his troops. In the old days, a number of post commanders took just such steps; the loss of business in town rapidly brought about a concession from the town folk or an acceptable compromise.

The list of community/military projects can go on and on. They can be quite elaborate—saluting a nearby city such as Savannah, Georgia, for which the commander of Fort Stewart, located a few miles away, arranged to have the Navy's Blue Angels and the Army's Golden Knights put on demonstrations and invited the city out to the post to witness them. However, a project can easily be more reasonable and inexpensive, such as a well-drilled platoon and/or the unit band to march in the local Fourth of July parade. The point is obvious: Army posts and nearby civilian communities need each other. And the Army must do its share, working with the local community, to ensure tranquility, harmony, and a decent atmosphere for its soldiers. To rephrase an old cliché: The road from post to town is very assuredly a two-way street.

Man is a competitive animal.

Competition

The youths of America are brought up on competition—in academic life, in athletics, in daily life. Television glorifies the winner whether in sports, guessing games, or soap operas. These days, the old saw "It's not whether you win or lose that counts; it's the way you play the game" has taken an about-face. Less cynically, however, we must conclude that healthy competition is a good thing for individuals and units.

In the 674th Airborne FA Battalion, we developed a "Best by Test" award, a simple streamer hung on the guidon of the firing battery scoring highest on the monthly battery firing tests. (The firing test was the standard battery ATT.) We also developed an administrative award to the battery that came out highest each month on various inspections—motor pools, day rooms, barracks, orderly rooms, supply rooms, messes, and so on. The competition between units was keen, and the improvement in all phases of battalion operations visible and measurable.

Another system used by one division commander in garrison—and in variation probably by all unit commanders—is the monthly meeting in which his staff shows charts illustrating a variety of measurements by major command. The statistics include AWOLs, MP reports, courts-martial, property losses, recruiting results, serious incidents, discharges of all kinds, or any other problem area. The commander needs to make few comments at these sessions because the indicators speak for themselves, and subordinate commanders can see where they have to improve. The charts definitely grab the subordinate commanders' attention.

Company and battery sports competition is also an excellent builder of morale and esprit. The men in a battalion or company,

61

particularly those who have been together for some time, are close-knit and cheer one another with enthusiasm.

Competition boosts the adrenalin of even hardened professional athletes who get "up" for a game against an arch rival. At the college level, a second-rate football team, trampled all year by the opposition, can rise to great heights against a national champion rival: Navy (the underdog) vs. Army in 1947.

Competition motivates an athlete. By the same token, it also inspires, stimulates, and impels a military organization to great feats on the field of battle. (Some of the competition in Vietnam, particularly measured by "body count," may have got out of hand. In World War II, General Patton was a master at pitting his subordinates one against another or pitting his whole Third Army against any other—particularly the Germans—during a fight.)

Sports and other events can motivate military units to great enthusiasm. The 674th and the 2d Battalion 187th occupied the two-battalion post at Camp Wood, Japan, after our return from Korea in November 1953. The two battalions had a very close rivalry in all matters: shenanigans at the Officers' and NCO Club, softball, parades, six-man football, even statistics of all kinds. The 674th formed its own drum and bugle corps because the RCT Band was at Beppu, Japan, ninety miles away and rarely available; the 2d/187th formed one also.

Ultimately, the CO of 2d/187th and I decided to schedule an athletic field day in which as many troops as possible could participate. We organized a tennis tournament, basketball and softball games, a platoon marching competition, and topped it off in the afternoon with a six-man tackle football game for which both battalions turned out en masse, one on one side and the other across the field. The drum and bugle corps played at halftime, the cheerleaders roused the troops, and the teams had at it with great enthusiasm. When the score was finally tallied at the end of the day (one point for each man participating on a winning team), I must regretfully report that the winner was the 2d Battalion 187th RCT. (My platoon's silent drill did me in.) Nonetheless, it was a great day. It showed what can be done for little or no money, and it paid great dividends in esprit, camaraderie, and unit cohesiveness. And the proof that it was a memorable day for the two battalions involved is that I can recall in detail many of the events some thirty years later.

And to prove that competition is far from dead in today's Army, a recent edition of the *Fort Bragg Paraglide* contained the following story under the headline, "Competition adds spice to training":

> Training, training, and more training can become tiresome, if not boring, when it seems repetitious. However, when competition is added to the tasks, it can be a different story.
>
> Company C, 307th Engineer Battalion, conducted a squad competition in 13 tasks, July 12–14.
>
> "With competition, each troop knows his squad is relying on him. Therefore, he is wide-awake and alert," said Capt. Ted Thomas, commander of Company C. "The squad works as a team and you get a lot of camaraderie."
>
> The competition included: a 10-kilometer run, setting up a triple standard concertina fence, a route reconnaissance, compass course, setting up a 292-radio antenna using proper procedures, making a target folder, setting up demolitions, making a one-rope bridge, emplacing a hasty protective mine field, removing a hasty mine field, vehicle inspection, equipment decontamination, and running through the team assault course.
>
> The events were scored based on a specific time limit, a written test on the task, and completing the task.
>
> Winning first place in the vehicle inspection, radio procedure, one-rope bridge, and land navigation helped the 3d Squad, 2d Platoon, to overall victory in the competition.
>
> "They were motivated throughout the events, and they gave it their best shot," said SSGT Russell G. Smith about his squad members. "We knew from the word go we'd be up there; why settle for second when you can be number one?"

And, as they say in the television commercials, "That says it all."

Chew in private, praise in public.

Credit

Napoleon once said that he could conquer Europe with a few yards of different colored ribbons that he would convert into awards for varying degrees of heroism and service and present them to his intrepid and merit-deserving officers and men at parades and other public spectacles.

Often we forget to praise and give credit. Kind words for a man who has done a good job cost nothing. Writing a letter of commendation to a man who has earned one is easy.

One battalion commander wrote to the wives or parents of his deserving young officers and men. Winning the hearts and minds of the young wives is one of the most important things we can do to retain in the Army the high-quality officer and NCO that we need and want.

Civilian workers on an installation need encouragement, too. Another commander made a point of going personally to the desk, workbench, or place of business of a member of his civilian work force to commend or reward him. This put the honoree among his peers when he was being honored, which understandably raised his chest a few notches.

At a staff conference one day, I mentioned that Colonel So-and-So had made a splendid short speech at an honor ceremony the preceding day. The colonel later told me that was the first time in his career that any commander had praised him publicly.

Other ways of praising deserving men are at retreat parades, honor ceremonies, staff meetings, morning parades, and company formations. The type of ceremony depends on the degree of the honor.

The converse—correct a man in private—is also true. No man wants to get chewed out in public in front of his peers. Reprimands are for the close confines of one's office or out of earshot of anyone else. The shorter and the more to the point the criticism, the better. One battalion commander (again, it was I) chewed out his motor officer, who had clearly neglected his duties (by not being present in the battalion area when the battalion returned from a week in the field), with the following: "You blew it. You let me and the battalion down. Now get out and get with it." (The chewee had the last word, though. He said, "Yes, sir.")

One must have enough self-confidence and understanding to be able to praise another. It's one of the most important traits a commander can have. But it is absolutely wrong to overdo it and praise those who do not deserve it. This dilutes the system, degrades subsequent plaudits, and negates the purpose of the award or praise.

(The Army is, apparently, still trying to crawl out from under the seemingly deserved criticism it received for the staggering number of medals and citations it awarded after the Grenada operation.)

Never make a decision you can't enforce.

Decisions

No matter how good your intentions, no matter how clear your thoughts are to you, no matter how much anguish, study, and analysis go into your decision making, if the decision is not clear or not enforceable, it's worse than worthless. On the other hand, procrastination, handwringing, soul-searching, and indecisiveness never accomplished a mission either.

Many of us have sat through so-called decision briefings, or have given them, only to find that the man who is to make the decision mumbles some unintelligible something-or-other and leaves the room. Then it's up to those remaining to try to figure out just what the decision was. (The higher the level of command, the more apt one is to run into this sort of ambiguous pronouncement.)

One case in point involved a very high ranking officer, who shall remain nameless, who never could deliver a clear, concise, decisive approval or disapproval at the end of a briefing. He hemmed and hawed, squirmed and wiggled, mumbled some innocuous, less-than-world-shaking statement, and finally strode regally from the room with the recommendations dangling in the air. (He may have epitomized the observation that some men get to the top by never making a mistake—because they never made a decision.) Then his staff had to figure out what to do next.

On the other hand, his successor, a hard-bitten, crusty, demanding, cantankerous fact-seeker, left no doubt in anyone's mind about his decisions. They were clear, to the point, and brief. He might have chewed up the briefer at some point during the presentation for a lack of facts or illogical conclusions. But at the end, there was a decision. Action officers respected and admired him because they knew exactly what he wanted and the direction that they were to take.

A decision must be enforceable—regardless of the level of command at which it is issued (squad to army). If it is not, the troops will pay very mixed attention to the order, and discipline will suffer.

No matter what kind of decision you are called upon to make, you must make certain that you know both sides of the story and that you have the facts. Then, and only then, can you decide what is best for the man, the unit, or the mission—whatever it may be. Justice, fairness, and compassion are the ingredients that, when mixed, form the basis for good decisions. Without them, you have unhappy troops, low morale, fractured discipline, and mission failure.

When you must make a decision contrary to a man's request, it is essential, when you can, to talk to him and explain why it was that you had to do what you did. You must, however, not let yourself get drawn into an argument once you have made your decision. This is why you must know the facts, both sides of the story, before you decide. Then stick with your decision.

Throughout a military career, one is called upon often to make decisions—some momentous, some routine and minor. But when they involve people, they're all important. A court-martial epitomizes the most balanced decision-making process: Both sides of the story have been researched, diagnosed, and then presented to the court, which must make a decision. Once, as a very young major just after World War II, I served on a court that sentenced a man to be "hanged by the neck until dead" for wartime desertion. In the end, he was not executed (to the best of my knowledge there was only one execution for desertion in World War II), but we had to assume that he would be. Making that kind of decision requires deep soul-searching.

Promotion boards are also arenas wherein the board members must make decisions that seriously affect a soldier's or officer's career. A board member has before him every recorded shred of biographical data about the nominees up for promotion. It's all laid out in each person's file. The hard part is sorting out the superior from the merely excellent. Probably the most difficult promotion board to serve on is the one that selects the annual brigadier general list. Superb colonels abound in the Army, and it is extremely challenging and laborious to cull out the water-walkers from the merely superior colonels.

But battery, company, and battalion commanders are required by the very nature of their jobs to make important decisions every waking moment. In combat, an ill-considered decision can cause needless loss of life. In garrison, an ill-considered decision can have far-reaching effects on a man's life or career. Thus, the commander must reason out his thoughts before making a decision, must weigh all the factors involved, even as in a court-martial where both sides of the story are presented. Then and only then can he make his decision.

In the worst kind of decision making, a commander makes a hasty but poor decision, someone on his staff with some nerve points out to him the fallacy of the decision and its undesirable consequences, and then he must either *(a)* let it stand to the disadvantage of someone (perhaps the whole unit), or *(b)* rescind the decision and start over. Far better to think it through from the beginning and then stand firm.

When the troops say a commander is "hard but fair," you know that commander makes good decisions.

They keep the top of the desk neat and tidy.

Desk Drawers

In these bureaucratic days, the lowest level administrator or staff officer has a desk. Occasionally, one should consider those other parts of the desk besides the top—the drawers.

One staff officer I knew had an almost psychotic penchant for a clean and clear desk top. He used his desk drawers for his in and out baskets, his pen sets, calendars, schedules, the works. Another one had a special drawer for notes he wrote to himself. Eventually, these notes formed the basis for his commanders and staff meeting. Still another officer, a four-star general, would write a note to himself when he had given a staff officer or commander a task and drop it into a desk drawer. Periodically, he reviewed the accumulation of notes and checked on the progress of his subordinates. The system made him, in the eyes of the subordinates unaware of the stashed memos, a mystical character with superhuman power of total recall and follow-up.

The real danger of desk drawers lies in their almost human ability to accumulate papers that should have been handled routinely months ago. One case illustrates the point: When DA teams were surveying finance offices worldwide to establish JUMPS (for the uninitiated, Joint Universal Military Pay System, an automated, quick-reaction, centrally operated system under which the Army is now paid), the teams routinely went through the desk drawers of the finance clerks to see what they could find. And they found plenty. They discovered all manner of misplaced allotment changes, promotion orders, leave papers, every kind of administrative matter affecting the pay of the troops. Naturally, thereafter the survey teams started their inspections with a thorough examination of the contents of finance clerks' desk drawers. The accuracy of JUMPS and its responsiveness to the problems of soldiers is at least partly attributable to this desk drawer–cleaning operation by the survey teams.

Desk drawers may seem to be innocuous, functional receptacles for all manner of odds and ends, junk, papers, cigarettes, note paper, pens, pencils, erasers, ad infinitum. They are not. Desk drawers hide Secret documents illegally held; they hide the books and magazine the user reads when the boss is out of the room; they conceal actions that are too tough or time-consuming for the occupant to do now.

I learned the hard way to keep my desk drawers in order. One day, while I was serving as an assistant secretary to the General Staff in the Pentagon (a lieutenant colonel slot), I came back to my office to find the Vice Chief of Staff sitting at my desk having a look through it to see what was deposited therein. One may think that this is an invasion of privacy, but I did not. Fortunately, the desk was in order, and the Vice Chief proceeded, with great non-chalance and aplomb, to carry on a conversation with me standing almost at attention in front of my own desk. (This is the same mis-chievous Vice Chief with whom, on occasion, one would find one-self eyeball to eyeball as one peeked through the slot in his office door to see if all was clear before entering. And on yet another ordinary day in the life of an Assistant SGS, as I was waiting to enter the Vice Chief's office, I saw smoke rings puffing from that same peephole as the Vice Chief blew his cigar smoke through the hole. Things were not always grim on the E Ring.)

The point is that one should always keep one's desk in order. It seems fairly accurate to conclude that a staff officer who has a desk cluttered with papers strewn like confetti all over it, with layers of files covering the desk, chairs, and cabinets, and with message forms all over the office must be either a genius or a man possessed of a very disorderly mind. Since there are very few of the former, one can only assume that the paper-scatterer is the latter. Perhaps this is faulty reasoning, but in many cases it holds true.

Desk drawers and desktops may be the private domain of the desk's occupant, but it is the wise commander and/or staff chief who checks the innards of desks—including his own—periodically.

There's no substitute for eyeball-to-eyeball contact.

Do It Yourself

The old rule that states that a commander or staff chief should get out and see for himself what is going on in his domain is as important today as it was in the era of horse artillery, semaphore flags, and campaign hats. Whether you are the Chief of Staff of the Army (who makes many trips all over the world to see for himself what the Army is up to), a sergeant commanding a squad, or a battalion staff officer, you must get out of the office, see what the unit is up to, and determine how well things are going in your bailiwick.

One division commander who was also an installation commander made daily morning visits to his troop units at their first morning formations (see Morning Parade) before he went to his own office. Then he followed up these visits with trips to various staff agencies at randomly selected buildings and activities (commissary, laundry, supply points, etc.) all over the post. During the day he visited units in the field. It made for a long day, but the commander was widely informed of the activities of the post and the subordinates were on their toes, never knowing when or where the boss might drop in. A battalion or company commander is in a perfect position to follow a similar routine.

Some commanders carry "do it yourself" pretty far. One, in Europe, wore mod clothes and a wig to check for discrimination in the places his troops frequented; another division commander, who looked rather young, often went in the field with no insignia so that the troops would be uninhibited in their talks with him.

Some commanders, particularly in their own vehicles and in civilian clothes, made a point of picking up troops from bus stops or ride points. They can learn a tremendous amount about local activities from their hitchhikers.

In addition to talking to troops and seeing for himself the state of training and morale, and the general condition of his unit, a commander must also get the feel and look of his unit activities. A commander who has fired all the weapons of his unit obviously has a great appreciation for what they can and cannot do; a staff officer who has followed requisitions from company level to supply point knows a lot about the whole logistics system; a commander who endures the hardships of his troops has an understanding of their problems and difficulties. Every staff officer and commander has an obligation to know his section and command intimately.

No staff reports, briefings, or phone conversations can ever substitute for what a man sees and feels when he goes to where the action is. And that is one of the most essential ingredients in commandership.

In 1971, when I commanded the Big Red One (BRO), we went to Europe on REFORGER. While there, the division came under the command of USAREUR. The deputy commanding general of USAREUR was Gen. "Ace" Collins, a highly respected three-star general famous for his training methods. Before he visited the Big Red One in its field locations, he would call ahead and ask that a driver and a jeep meet him at a specified heliport. He would take care of himself from then on, he would add. He made it perfectly clear that he wanted neither me nor a staff officer to accompany him, knowing full well that we would lead him to the places we wanted him to see and avoid the places and units we wished to hide. Thus, General Collins saw all the warts and bruises as well as the more presentable aspects of the BRO in the field in Germany. His method saved me time, it avoided interfering with the activities of the units, and it obviously gave General Collins a firsthand, honest look at the BRO.

Prince Charles of England, whose visits and itineraries are carefully published and planned well in advance, complains that his nostrils are constantly bruised by the smell of fresh paint. General Collins's system for visiting and inspecting the troops negates all that last-minute spit and polish, paint and whitewash that greets Prince Charles at every stop.

When President Kennedy visited Fliegerhorst Kaserne during his celebrated visit to Europe in 1963, we were required by a CG with a well-known penchant for neatness, shine, and glisten to paint only that portion of the hangars that the president could see during his ride-by. (We also had to save money.) There is no doubt that spit and polish have their place in the scheme of things military, but white-washed stone path markers, painted grass, and half-painted buildings may be carrying things a bit too far.

NCOs, captains, lieutenant colonels in the chain of command need to get out of their offices and see for themselves what's going on with their troops. And they should always be on the alert during a guided tour. COs, if accompanied by subordinate commanders, should always veer off the scheduled path and look behind the barracks, check the rear of maintenance shops, and wander innocently into the normally unvisited places. Ah, the revelations that come to light, the hidden problems that are unearthed, the symbolic dirty laundry that falls out of unlikely spots. This procedure may be diabolical, but it certainly gets results and spawns red-faced and chagrined, but suddenly educated, subordinates.

The Army has devised thousands of reports to relay information up the chain. There are inspectors at all levels to check compliance with various regulations. There are staff officers whose duties encompass staff visits, reports, and briefings to the commander. But none of these is a substitute for the commander's getting away from his desk, visiting his units, talking to his troops, listening to their comments, inspecting their living conditions, checking the mess at unusual times, and seeing for himself what is going on in his outfit.

This is especially true the higher up the ladder one progresses. A man can listen to innumerable briefings and discussions on a given subject, but if he does not go to the scene of the action, he has no clear-cut idea of what it is all about. (Obviously, this is especially true in combat.)

Take, for example, a battalion maintenance shop. It doesn't take a maintenance expert to be able to look around a shop and decide whether or not it is efficiently organized and run. The location of the work areas, the proximity of the tools, their condition and sufficiency, the system for controlling repair parts, the arrangement of work priority, the assignment of jobs, the work hours, the distractions from the maintenance job itself—all of those can be checked by a commander even if he is in a hurry.

Unscheduled command visits have many ancillary rewards. Primarily, they help a commander get to know his men, they help him discover for himself how the troops are living, and they assist him in uncovering the deficiencies in his organization. These are compelling reasons for every commander to get out and see for himself and then take the necessary corrective action.

Briefings, Fort Riley, Kansas. U.S. Army photo

Solutions are far more complicated than the problem.

Drugs

One usually sees a discussion such as this headed "Drug and *Alcohol* Abuse Problem." Alcohol is a drug and, therefore, need not be singled out from the hundreds of other varieties of drugs that all strata of society use and abuse. Alcohol abuse is simply more accepted in our society than is drug abuse. But the number of deaths caused annually by drunken drivers in the United States is hardly a reassuring statistic for this socially acceptable aberration. Until we all accept the fact that alcohol is a drug, the solution to the total problem is much more difficult.

I include this discussion because all levels of command must be concerned with the problem—the lower the level, the more important the concern. And my experience at the division level has value, I think, throughout the whole structure.

In early 1971, all of us who were in command positions in the Army were, then as now, groping with the problems of drugs. We had by then recognized that we had a problem of great proportions on our hands, that we could no longer ignore it, and that we "had to do something about it." In those days, the attempt at a solution centered around what was then a radical approach: the establishment of Sunshine Houses, or other euphemistically named places, where a drug-addicted or drug-dependent man could go for help or where his friends could take him when he was suffering a bad trip and was unable to go on his own.

The places were staffed with psychologists, psychiatrists, and occasionally (theoretically) reformed addicts, who acted as guidance counselors, sympathizers, and staffers for the centers. Usually, in those days, the counselors were in mod civilian clothes, their hair was inordinately long, and they tried to be part of the scene. The centers themselves were decorated with posters, the walls were covered with graffiti of varying kinds, they were dimly lighted, and the furniture was low and makeshift, often simply mattresses on the floors. There was, of course, the inevitable crash pad for the bad tripper.

As an installation commander, I established such a center and considered that I was in the forefront of the leaders who were "doing something about the drug problem."

I got a rude comeuppance from a young black woman who accompanied a higher headquarters drug survey team to the installation. After the team's survey of our situation, she told me that I was going about the problem in the wrong manner, that rather than dissuading the drug abuser by providing him with such a setup, I was, in fact, simply giving him a legitimized place, on post, where he could meet other drug abusers, and where he would feel at home. This was the wrong approach, said she, for there was nothing in the setup to cause the abuser to want to get off whatever he was on and clean up himself and his system; there was no discipline, no structure, nothing to cause the man to want to come back to the real world.

The next day I closed the place, much to the opposition and chagrin of my counselors and psychiatrist. The Engineers repainted the interior, hauled out the ratty furniture and junky fixtures, and established a booth for each counselor. I had the staff get regulation haircuts, put on their uniforms, and furnish their counseling cubicles very simply with a desk and chair and a straight-backed chair for the client. We kept records. In fact, thereafter, we put the whole operation on an almost clinical basis.

We used counseling, advice, sympathy, and education about the perils of drugs. We tried to find and solve the problem a man may have had that caused him to take drugs in the first place. By close coordination with the first sergeants, we scheduled follow-up appointments and made certain that the men showed up.

We also established a halfway house where men who were on the road to recovery lived in a very regimented and disciplined atmosphere after duty hours. This required close supervision, of course. But it started them back on the road to discipline, structured living, and a willingness to rejoin their units.

The results are hard to assess. Which system is better for curing a man is, of course, debatable. There is no doubt in my mind, however, that my reformed system was far better. (Incidentally, how does one ever determine if a man is cured of drug abuse?)

The structured approach to the problem did give us a far better idea of what we were doing, it put the troops on notice that we meant business, and it made the whole system much easier to control.

And if all else fails and the drug user does not respond to treatment, waste no more time. Throw him out of the Army forthwith. We waste too much time as it is with drug users.

We had much more success with the alcohol abuse part of the problem. A very competent and wise chaplain set up an alcohol abuse program whereby he brought offenders into a specially set-aside ward of the hospital for a drying-out period of about three or four days. Then we had them report back in the evenings, two or three times a week, with their wives, if married (and our experience was that the alcohol abuser was an older man, married, seemingly more mature than the younger drug abuser), at periodic intervals for counseling, discussions, help, and follow-up. Many confirmed ex-problem drinkers are among his successes.

We also established a chapter of Alcoholics Anonymous on the post. AA does great work with alcoholics and did so for us.

There have been many commissions appointed to study the problem of drug and alcohol abuse, many staff agencies set up to handle the problem, many papers written on the subject, many lectures given by reformed drug addicts, many rap sessions held to discover ways to get at this diabolical, insidious issue.

The discussion here represents only one approach and one experience. It is by no means offered as a cure-all. The enormity of the problem defies limitation or structuring or design. But it requires a try. How much try is another question. We may be expending prodigious resources to reclaim only a very small percentage of hard-drug addicts. Even long established sanatoriums have achieved only very limited success.

Nonetheless, officers and NCOs at the battalion level have a special responsibility to their men to assist them in getting rid of their drug and alcohol difficulties. Ignoring the problems or "sweeping them under the rug" is without merit. The young leaders must know exactly what the post offers for handling drug and alcohol abuse problems and then insist that those troops in need of help avail themselves of it. We cannot view and treat the problems with "benign neglect" or stupid indifference. The issue is far too rampant, costly, and unit-degrading to ignore.

Education is one of the greatest benefits of the Army.

Education

The educational opportunities that the Army offers a man in its ranks are almost limitless. They go beyond purely on-the-job training and experience; a soldier can become a communications expert, a medical or dental technician, a mechanic, a demolitions specialist, a clerk, a computer wizard, or a carpenter (even an infantryman, a tanker, or a redleg) or learn any of a myriad skills and professions that equip a soldier for excellent jobs in the civilian world after his enlistment or career is over. The opportunities go beyond the learning associated with maturing in the Army, learning to live with one's fellow man or woman, developing self-discipline, leading others, and accomplishing missions varying from simple leadership tasks to the heaviest of responsibilities in combat. An ambitious man or woman can even progress from non–high school graduate to Ph.D. while in the Army or under the Army's auspices.

I knew an intelligent, ambitious young man who was about to get out of the Army. He had been my driver at Fort Bragg for about a year. He could have become a senior NCO far faster than his age group if he had decided to stay in. But he wanted two things: to fly and to get an education. Therefore, before he left the Army, he went through Project Transition, and he learned to fly a small airplane. He was so good at it that he stayed on at the flying school after his discharge, became an instructor, and earned his instrument ticket. Then he went off to college on the G.I. Bill. He graduated from college *magna cum laude* while holding a job at night to help finance his education and support his family. Then he applied for and was accepted into the Regular Navy for flight training. Eventually, he became a full lieutenant flying jets from carriers and during his off-duty hours earned two master's degrees, one in business administration. This is probably an exceptional case but certainly not an isolated one.

79

Take the case of a man who was smart and ambitious and decided to make a career of the Army. Thirty years ago, he entered the Army just out of high school. Over the years he obtained a commission, got his college diploma, graduated from Harvard with a Ph.D. in business administration, and rose to the rank of major general, Regular Army, before retirement. This again shows the Army's ability to help those who want to take advantage of all that the Army offers.

Then there's the extreme case of the present Chairman of the Joint Chiefs of Staff, Gen. John W. Vessey, Jr. His career is a legendary rags to riches—or bars to stars—tale. As a young enlisted man in World War II, General Vessey hit every rank from private to first sergeant. At Anzio, this twenty-one-year-old first sergeant won a battlefield commission as a second lieutenant. Thereafter, his promotions came generally with his peers—until he reached the rank of colonel. Throughout his early career, General Vessey took full advantage of all the Army's educational opportunities. He finished college and thereafter worked for and received a master's degree. He attended all the Army's succession of schools through the War College. In Vietnam, he received the D.S.C. for uncommon valor. Once he was selected for brigadier general, the speed of his promotions stepped up, until finally even the president recognized his worth and named him Chairman of the Joint Chiefs.

These examples perhaps dwell on the exceptional. But the Army does offer innumerable courses for soldiers to hone their specialties and learn new ones if they are interested enough to ask for and pursue the opportunity.

Consider what the government does for a soldier after his enlistment. The Veterans Educational Assistance Program (VEAP) will match a soldier's savings for college two for one, up to a maximum of $5,400. Any two-, three-, or four-year enlistee can sign up for the program and have $8,100 for college if he saves a maximum of $2,700 during his tour ($2,400 during a two-year tour).

Then there's the Army College Fund. If a soldier's AFQT Score is 50 or better and he enlists in one of the Army's critical skills, he gets not only the $5,400 from VEAP but also a kicker of $12,000 for a three- or four-year enlistment. And if he enlists for four years in infantry, armor, or artillery, he receives a $5,000 bonus that he need not apply to college. Thus, a three-year enlistee could be discharged with $20,100, and a four-year enlistee with $25,100, toward his college education. That should just about see him through.

Additionally, the Army will pay 75 percent of the cost of off-duty training for a soldier in local technical or regular colleges and will see to it that a soldier completes his GED for high school equivalency if at all possible.

The point is that every leader should find out about the possibilities that exist either on his post or at the "trade schools" for the education of his troops—either on or off duty. He should then encourage his soldiers to take full advantage of the opportunities and help them to achieve their goals. In the many surveys that try to find out what it is that the troops want most from the Army, the chance to complete their education invariably looms high. The best soldiers are obviously the best-educated ones. Education is good for the soldier, it is good for the Army, and therefore it is good for the country.

Efficiency Reports

Over the years, the Army has changed its efficiency report formats at increasingly shorter intervals, or so it would seem. Some of the changes have probably been initiated because the personnel managers wanted to capture more information about an officer's performance of duty, his job description, the number of days he spent on that job, his additional duties, and so on. In later years, however, OER formats have been changed probably because rating and endorsing officers had inflated the previous ones to meaninglessness.

For some reason, we in the Army (as opposed to the other services and other branches of government or industry) have a penchant for inordinately praising our subordinates, with the obvious result that reports suffer from inflation. It therefore becomes extremely hard for selection boards to discriminate between officers and NCOs, and selection for promotion, schools, command assignments, and staff positions becomes increasingly difficult.

A few officers have records that are singularly outstanding; these officers are readily recognized by a selection board. But they are a small percentage of the whole. Another few officers have records that are singularly bad; these, too, are easily identified by a board. But they, too, make up only a relatively small percentage of the total. Thus, a selection board is left with the job of culling out and making their selections from the large mass between those two extremes. And if the board makes mistakes, it is because of the efficiency report system.

In the early days of the Army, rating officers told it like it was. In 1813, Col. Lewis Cass, a regimental commander, submitted the following report:

Lower Seneca Town, August 15, 1813
Sir:

I forward a list of the officers of the ——th Regt. of Infty.— arranged agreeable to rank. Annexed thereto you will find all the observations I deem necessary to make.

Respectfully, I am, Sir,
Yo. Obt. Sevt.,
Lewis Cass
——th Regt. Infantry

Alexander Brown, Lt. Col., Cmdg.—A good-natured man.

Clark Crowell, 1st Major—A good man, but no officer.

Jess B. Wordsworth, 2nd Major—An excellent officer.

Captain Shaw—A man of whom all unite in speaking ill.

Captain Thomas Lord—Indifferent, but promises well.

Captain Rockwell—An officer of capacity, but imprudent and a man of violent passions.

Capt. Dan L. Ware
Capt. Parker
1st Lt. Jas. Kearns
} Strangers but little known in the regiment.

1st Lt. Thomas Dearfoot
1st Lt. Wm. Herring
1st Lt. Danl. Land
1st Lt. Jas. L. Bryan
1st Lt. Robert McKewell
} Low, vulgar men, with the exception of Herring. From the meanest walks of life—possessing nothing of the character of officers and gentlemen.

1st Lt. Robert Cross—Willing enough—has much to learn—with small capacity.

2nd Lt. Nicholas Farmer—A good officer, but drinks hard and disgraces himself and the Service.

2nd Lt. Stewart Berry—An ignorant unoffending fellow.

2nd Lt. Darrow—Just joined the Regiment—of fine appearance.

2nd Lt. Pierce
2nd Lt. Thos G. Slicer
2nd Lt. Oliver Warren
} Raised from the ranks, but all behave well and promise to make excellent officers.

2nd Lt. Royal Gore
2nd Lt. Means
2nd Lt. Clew
2nd Lt. McLear
} All promoted from the ranks, low, vulgar men, without one qualification to recommend them—more fit to carry the hod than the epaulette.

2nd Lt. John G. Sheaffer—Promoted from the ranks. Behaves well.

Ensign Behan—The very dregs of the earth. Unfit for anything under the sun.

Ensign John Breen
Ensign Byor
} Promoted from the ranks—men of no manner and no promise.

Ensign North—From the ranks. A good young man who does well.

I quote this list to show that at least in the early days of the Army one commander told it as he saw it.

Much later, 1970 to be more exact, one of my commanders rated one of his subordinates as follows: "This officer has stacked arms." That was the entire narrative part of the report and nothing else obviously needed to be said. Another report, rendered by a four-star general on a major general, said: "This is the best major general in the Army." Period. End of report. But that's clear, concise, and pointed. It says it all. (That major general eventually became the Army Chief of Staff.)

Sometimes rating officers trip themselves up with misguided attempts at rhetoric. Here are some gems culled from recent reports:

No detail was too small for him to overlook.
Major ———, through stoic efforts ———.
Colonel W—— is one of those rare "head and shoulders" officers.

Some other rating and endorsing officers find the English language insufficient to their task. And so they confuse, mumble, and twist their words almost to the point of unintelligibility.

Someone, who is anonymous, but most probably was a red-eyed, caffeine-alert promotion board member, collected a list of gems from efficiency reports more recent, obviously, than those from Lower Seneca Town. The excerpts could have been from today or World War I or Teddy Roosevelt's Chargers. For what they are worth—and I think that they are priceless, not only for their double-talk, innuendo, ineptness, and inapplicability, but also for what they can teach today's raters—here are a few of the worst. (Obviously, these are simply excerpts—not the complete report, as was the case with the Lower Seneca gems.)

Some raters seem to have been influenced by a subordinate's alcoholic predilections:

His drinking habits are below minimum.
Drinks and holds it like a good recon man.
His one fault is his overfondness for drinking beer, however his duty never interfered in this.
Intemperate use of alcohol has prejudiced my evaluation in Section F.

There has been a marked improvement in this officer's use of alcoholic beverages.

Other raters have a penchant for describing an officer's interest in the opposite sex:

Conducts himself properly in sexual relations.

God's gift to women.

He has allowed himself to become entangled in a web of romantic problems to an extent that they must be considered chronic rather than unusual.

Appears to be a temporarily confirmed bachelor. While he is socially inclined and active, he is not prone to enter into entangling alliances with the female sex.

Some raters get carried away with words:

His turpitude is a source of satisfaction.

Handicapped by coccidoidemycosis.

Completed battle inoculation. [Well, maybe he did]

Likes peridontis.

Oversolicitousness for welfare of his men occasionally results in buying a "skinny pig in a fat poke."

A superior officer by any reasonable standards.

He has failed despite the opportunity to do so.

Recommend promotional status to next higher grade.

A grand chap but he is in too deep.

Then there are those raters who seem to dwell, however vaguely, on a ratee's physical or mental characteristics:

Has bad feet, easily frozen.

Has black hair.

Combs his hair to one side and appears rustic.

A tired old man.

A tall beautiful blond. [sex unspecified]

Has a prominent forehead.

A heavily built officer with smooth features and a conversational voice.

Limps on one leg.

A particularly fine appearance when astride a horse.

Captain ——— is a lanky officer whose thin face would be dominated by a Roman nose were it not for his calm, attentive and confident eyes. They are the eyes of a man who has taken a long-range view and has prepared himself for the long pull.

He is neat appearing except for his mustache.

A tall, stocky officer.

He is completely bald and this condition detracts from his military bearing.

All wool and a yard wide.

Some raters describe a subordinate's religious habits:

Seldom misses church on Sunday.

Believes sincerely in the power of prayer, and it is astonishing to note how many times his prayers are answered.

He is a good organizer, but leans a little on the Lord to get the work done.

Some raters describe an officer's personality and traits of character in various ways—sometimes obscure, sometimes obvious:

Tends to create the impression of unpositive personality through needless and undiscerning gentility and soft-spokenness.

He is quiet and reserved in manner, but always the gentleman in mind and carriage.

A hard-headed "redhead" who sometimes turns purple in an argument. His country-boy-come-to-town approach, combined with an ever-present name-brand cigar and "buck-toothed" grin has made him a mainstay for morale within the organization.

His leadership is outstanding except for his lack of ability to get along with subordinates.

A medium personality.

A quiet, reticent, neat-appearing officer. Industrious, tenacious, diffident, careful, and neat. I do not wish to have this officer as a member of my command at any time.

He hasn't any mental traits.

Is reluctant to have his opinion changed.

This officer has become an expert at sitting around and doing nothing. I have to rate her low due to her failure to perform her duties satisfactorily.

Needs careful watching since he borders on the brilliant.

He will work 12 to 16 hours a day unless actively engaged, which is not found in but few officers.

Of average intelligence except for lack of judgment on one occasion in attempting to capture a rattlesnake, for which he was hospitalized.

He consumes incredible amounts of Coca-Cola daily.

Uses colloquialisms.

Can express a sentence in two paragraphs anytime.

Ardent crossword puzzle fan.

And then, finally, comes the rater who must have been drafting his efficiency reports at the end of a long, miserable day. He writes:

Some are critical of an officer who delegates authority. Others criticize the officer who does not. Seldom does rater take into consideration the calibre of individuals to whom he would have to delegate his authority.

That kind of reporting is of little help to selection boards, although it may prove that the lives of raters, ratees, and selection board members are far from easy.

Unfortunately, frankness, openness, candor, brutal honesty, objectivity, and clarity do not find their way into all of our efficiency reports. Too many men have been dubbed water-walkers when we know that there are only a few who have sauntered across the Potomac. Even Washington had to cross the Delaware by boat, and God had to part the waters of the Red Sea to let Moses lead his people out of bondage in Egypt.

It's obviously difficult to write an objective report critical of a subordinate who has worked hard, has done some excellent work, and who should be rewarded. One also knows that the rated officer is going to see his report and find out what one thought of him. This is especially trying if one is basically "a nice guy." Part of the problem, however, is that inflation tends to beget inflation. The rater of a man who is outstanding and who the rater believes should eventually be a general goes all out in his prose to paint the picture of a man among men, a leader par excellence, a "truly outstanding" staffer, commander, organizer, and so on, and so on, who can "do it all." The rater feels that if he does not extol his virtues singularly, the rated officer will miss out for selection. And so it goes, inflation compounding inflation.

The problem can be solved only through honesty in reporting, a willingness to say exactly what you think of a subordinate—outlining his weaknesses as well as his solid points—and the recognition that not every man is destined to be, or should be, a general, or even a colonel.

Another point for commanders, at least from division level on down, is for the commander to rate or endorse those subordinate officers two levels down. Thus, division commanders would endorse battalion commanders and brigade commanders would endorse the company commanders in his brigade. The battalion commander should certainly endorse his platoon leaders. This accomplishes a lot of worthwhile things: It keeps the chain of command intact; it requires the commanders to get to know well two levels of their subordinate commanders; it probably introduces into the system an objectivity that might otherwise be missing if the rating officer were too close to his subordinates.

Efficiency reports may be a misnomer; one should also remember that inefficiency is also reportable.

Engineers may be too smart.

Engineers

At West Point, at least in fairly recent "old days," the graduating cadets select their arm or branch of service based upon their academic standing in the class. Thus, the number one cadet, academically, has his choice of almost any arm or branch of the Army. Then the succeeding cadets select their branches according to the quotas that remain. The last man in the class therefore is "ranked" into whatever one slot is left. Invariably, the highest ranking cadets select the Engineers. That branch, with smart cadets and ROTC students who have majored in engineering, is thus filled with brilliant, well-educated officers. This is all well and good, but in my non-engineer view, it may lead to some difficulties.

Some situations, such as post maintenance, do not require brilliant engineers. Some time ago, I inspected the renovation of a gym on a local post. The newly constructed part of the gym was fairly well done. But the renovated part left something to be desired. For example, the contract called for the basketball court floor to be resanded and varnished, but said nothing about the marred and dirty walls and pillars surrounding the floor.

The contract likewise directed the resanding of the floors of the squash and handball courts; it made no provision, however, for replacing rotten boards just outside the court, repairing the cracked and crumbling walls, or repainting them. And, unbelievably (at least to a handball player), the contract provided that the walls of the two new handball courts be painted gray.

On another post, the location for the new PX, commissary, bank, and other facilities to serve the troops and their families had originally been sited in an open space in the family housing area that would be surrounded by houses, would have no room for expansion, and would have no space for adequate parking. (This decision was not entirely the fault of the Engineers.) It didn't take a genius to figure out that the proper place for such a group of facilities should be between the troop and housing areas, where it would be within walking distance of the troop barracks, where there would be adequate space for expansion and for parking, and where it would also be convenient to the family housing area.

My horrible example (I hope overdone—but I wouldn't bet on it) has to do with the post engineer maintenance. This group is a predominantly civilian work force that has been on the job for years and years. Whenever some maintenance has to be done on a set of quarters or on some barracks, the procession begins. First, some sort of a supervisor and his helper, armed with the requisite work order (which has wound its way through a bureaucratic labyrinth), come to survey the job. This is a very lengthy process, even though it may involve simply painting a door, replacing a window-pane, or fixing an electrical outlet. Then they disappear and the work crew, after considerable delay and additional phone calls, appears to do the job. Four men are often assigned to paint the door, for example. After their arrival and their survey, there is the inevitable return of one man to the shop to get the paint or to get the right color of paint. The other three then sit around drinking coffee they have had sense enough to bring with them. Meanwhile, the errand boy returns with the paint or the proper tool or what-ever, and with any luck, the work begins. But by this hour it may be their quitting time, which is always considerably before the end of the day because the work team (this is a very loose description) must return to the shop, wash up, change clothes, empty their thermos bottles, discuss the day's activities, turn in the usual paperwork, and get ready to spring out the door (their only energetic activity of the day) just as the first note of the whistle blows. Unfortunately, I do not exaggerate.

But, fortunately, there are solutions. In the first place, any design engineer should very carefully go over his plans with an expert on the subject. The gym rehabilitation I mentioned would never have been planned the way it was if someone familiar with the inner workings of a gymnasium had looked at the plans or been consulted on them. The community facilities would never have been located where they were in the second example if a troop commander had looked at the master plan. All this suggests that what is needed on the staff of post engineers, design engineers, and district engineers is a reasonably dumb but logical mind that can cut through all of the engineer talk and plans and get to the heart of the matter. Failing that, someplace in the approval chain for engineer projects should be an expert in the field. (For example, an experienced motor officer should look at the design of a battalion maintenance shop.)

The solution to the lethargy, ineptness, and oversupervision of post maintenance crews is also relatively easy. These are the steps taken by a former commander of Fort Campbell:

1. He required the cross-training of all maintenance men so that one man could answer about 95 percent of the calls. Thus, one man could pass reasonably well as a plumber, electrician, carpenter, painter, or mason.

2. He took away the trucks that carried the crews on their rounds and issued his cross-trained men a three-wheeled scooter fitted out with a toolbox that carried a variety of supplies and tools. This cut crew sizes down to one and saved on gasoline and vehicle costs.

3. He required that the men make their rounds at the posted speed limits and not drive at 5 mph from place to place as had been their practice in the past.

4. He required that supervisors make their estimates by themselves, without the inevitable aide to assist and carry notebook, pencil, and paperwork.

5. He established quotas of work and required that they be met.

6. And finally, he set up a store in the housing area where the men of the households could draw repair parts, light bulbs, paint, tools, washers, and the like to do the work on their quarters themselves.

I know another post commander (me, again) who permitted the post engineer to repaint the interior of quarters, when necessary, any color the occupant wanted—so long as that color was off-white. The women of the post actually loved it because the curtains, drapes, rugs, and so on, that they had brought from a previous set of quarters would inevitably harmonize with a house whose walls were off-white.

For the record, let it be known that engineers do many great tasks, efficiently, cheaply, and well. After all, Army engineers did build the Panama Canal, they did explore the West, they did lay out and install the railroads across the plains, they do run our harbors and ports, they do develop and manage our water resources, and they performed miracles of construction in all of our wars. In addition, they built the Pentagon in an unbelievably short time, the Saint Lawrence Seaway, huge dams on the Columbia and Missouri rivers, the atomic bomb, the Alcan Highway, and the Ledo and Burma roads, to mention just a few of their tremendous achievements. That's what they need the "smarts" for.

But let it also be said that sometimes their ingenious minds overlook the obvious. That's why we need to salt a few less than brilliant but logical types to work with them.

(I've included this section because captains, majors, and lieutenant colonels inevitably are forced out of command positions and must take onerous staff jobs. But even as company and battalion commanders, they must deal with post engineers. Forewarned is forearmed, as some nonengineer type once said.)

You can't touch it, but you can feel it.

Esprit de Corps

The Red Devils of the British 1st Airborne Division, battered, besieged, and decimated by S.S. troops and the panzer units of Hitler's forces outside Arnhem in the grim days of 1944, refused to surrender to the overwhelming German forces that surrounded them. The Red Devils hung on in the face of merciless, devastating, incessant attacks.

Brig. Gen. Anthony McCauliffe, the commander of the American 101st Airborne Division, surrounded by the Germans at Bastogne, was called upon by Gen. Smilo von Luettwitz to surrender. General McCauliffe answered briefly and emphatically, "Nuts." The Germans thought this was simply a very cryptic reply until they realized it meant, "Go to Hell."

A company of American soldiers, led by a small, tough young captain wearing a battered Luxembourg dress cap in the middle of combat in the dark days of the Korean retreat, held on to its position in the face of overwhelming attacks led by the Chinese "volunteers."

The history of military warfare is replete with similar examples of courage, dedication, resolution, motivation, sacrifice, loyalty, and faith. More simply stated, that's "esprit de corps." As the dictionary defines it, it is "a common spirit of devotion and enthusiasm among members of a group for one another, their group, and its purposes."

Esprit de corps is the end-all of discipline, training, and education of a unit. It is the goal of all commanders and, for that matter, of the managers of factories, stores, firms, and athletic teams. It comes from the knowledge that one's outfit, be it a football team, a Volvo plant, a franchise for McDonald's hamburgers, has an important job to do, that the members of the outfit are well trained, and that they are the best there is at whatever it is that they are doing. It comes from having a faith and belief in one's mission and that one is expected to do well and to act often "above and beyond the call of duty." It is the belief that one is of the elite and will not let such an outfit down. It comes from leaders who take care of their men. It comes from loyalty up as well as down. It comes from knowing the men in one's unit. It comes from believing that the cause is right and the goal proper. It comes from identifying oneself with the rest of the unit. It comes from the competitive instinct to win at whatever one is doing. It comes from caring.

It does not come from pay raises, fancy barracks, or outlandishly expensive mess halls. As a matter of fact, esprit seems to thrive in adversity, grow when the odds are the slimmest, and climax when all seems hopeless. The men with the toughest jobs to do have an almost inherent sense of esprit. A unit under fire, living in the mud, short of rations, isolated, and cold may have far greater esprit than a unit in the rear area of the combat zone living in heated billets, eating three hot meals a day, staying warm, riding to work—and with little to do but bitch about their conditions.

At one point during World War II, I was the XO of a parachute field artillery battery. We were in the throes of getting ready to deploy overseas, prior to which we had to endure a command inspection of all of our equipment. This meant that some equipment had to be painted, wooden items had to be sanded, aluminum pots and pans had to be steel-wooled, and everything else had to be either oiled, scraped, sandpapered, or hidden (definitely verboten). We also had to endure predeployment movies and lectures on any subject the War Department thought we needed to help us survive, settle our account, understand censorship, identify bugs, and hate the Germans and the Japs.

Prior to one of these movies, my battery was sanding and scraping our D-handled shovels. The work was not progressing with much speed or enthusiasm, so I got a shovel and proceeded to work on it, informing the section that I hadn't gone to West Point for four years to learn how to scrape a shovel, and I wanted them to get with the action. They fell to with a much better attitude. Later at the theater during a yawn-producing lecture the entire battalion had to attend, there came from the back of the theater the constant noise of scraping, with an occasional banging of metal on the floor and a rasping, nerve-tingling sound. The battalion commander sent a staff officer to investigate the disturbance. That worthy gentleman reported that the men of C Battery had brought their shovels to the theater and were passing the time getting them ready for the upcoming command inspection. The battalion commander merely shook his head in silence, as if to say, "What in the hell will they think of next?" He did not order me to have the men cease and desist. He understood. I feel that there was a little more esprit built up in that unit by that single incident. The men could tell the story and embellish it for months.

Paratroopers, Green Berets, Rangers, pilots, Navy frogmen, demolition teams, all have a built-in ingredient for developing esprit de corps. In such units you can see and feel the esprit: Men strut, they speak with confidence, they stand tall, they act like soldiers, they have high morale, they attack their missions—combat or otherwise—with enthusiasm, boldness, and self-reliance. They know they are good, that their mission is important, that they are critical parts of a crucial military team.

But what of other units less significantly endowed with a built-in esprit generator? They, too, can have great esprit and unit pride. It may be that a charismatic commander can pull an outfit together by sheer dint of his personality; it may be a unique mission that lends esprit to a unit; it may be an athletic victory by a service unit over, say, a parachute outfit, that gives the service unit pride and self-respect—important parts of esprit de corps. And it is esprit de corps that causes units to face overwhelming odds and yet proceed, undaunted, with their missions. The Light Brigade at Balaklava in the Crimean War in 1854, the Red Devils at Arnhem in 1944 and the 101st Airborne at Bastogne in December 1944 are exemplary illustrations. But esprit need not be associated only with units; witness the self-respect, self-pride, and self-discipline of our POWs under the notorious torture of the Japanese, the North Koreans, and particularly the Vietnamese.

All these examples point out that esprit de corps is possible in any unit; but that to achieve it, a unit and its men, individually and collectively, must be challenged; they must be given tough jobs; they must know that they and their unit are important; and they must know and feel that their leaders believe in them.

Esprit de corps, that elusive pot of gold at the end of a commander's rainbow, results.

Keeping troops informed, 5/16 Infantry air mobile assault. U.S. Army photo

KISS—Keep It Simple, Stupid.

Euphemisms

In all of the outfits or staff agencies of which I have been a part
(especially so since I have become a general), I have insisted on
acceptance of my counterpart of two more famous rules of operation, the Peter Principle and Murphy's Law. For want of a better
name, I call my rule the Flanagan Formula. Simply stated, it is
this: If Flanagan can understand it, anyone can.

Earlier, in the chapter on Communications, I aired some of
my petulance about the tortured, ambiguous, and circumlocutory
words, phrases, and constructions that are passing for the English
language these days. The Army, unfortunately, is as guilty as its
civilian counterparts of double-talk, confusion, and obfuscation.
At the risk of being repetitious, I feel compelled to take the Army's
phrase-makers to task for, among many others, the following
attempts to disguise some of the Army's hallowed institutions,
operations, and people.

New Army Speak	Translation
counter indiscipline index	punishment rate
human resources	people
blue-collar supervisor	foreman
recreation services	special services
human resources development	leadership (loosely)
music and theater program	entertainment
sports and athletic training program	sports
dining facility	mess hall
dining facility supervisor	mess sergeant
denture obstruction extractor	toothpick

The list could go on *ad nauseum.*

Why must we use civilian jargon? Why must we give up our

traditional and commonly accepted, easily understood terms? (I know why: It's because of the civilian bureaucrats and officers who have earned their M.A.s, M.S.s and Ph.D.s in civilian institutions.)

Does changing the name of an agency make it better? Does calling a mess hall a dining facility improve the chow? Is a group supervisor a better leader than a platoon sergeant?

An installation supervisor is still the post commander. A personnel manager is still the G-1 or S-1. My recommendation is this: Stop fiddling with the time-honored and accepted terms that everyone understands and get on with the job of training soldiers to fight and win battles. (For the benefit of those bureaucrats who cannot understand that clause "to fight and win battles," I'll translate: To deploy an array of work groups of various organization and management concepts against a similarly arrayed but hostile and antagonistic force. The management objective of the first force is to cause the second group both to abandon its work implements and to effect a retrograde movement organizationally disrupted and management voided.)

Just what does this discussion have to do with platoon sergeants, company commanders, and battalion commanders? It has this to do with them: They should be aware of what is happening to the military language that, in its traditional sense, was clear, to the point, and understandable by the rank and file as well as the colonels and generals. They should avoid jargon of the bureaucrats and stick to their time-tested military vocabulary. They should teach their troops that same language. They should, in short, be military.

*A unit does well those things the commander
checks.*   Gen. Bruce Clark

Follow-Up

Two of the most important precepts I learned as a young lieutenant were these: Never try personally to handle a drunken soldier,
and never give an order you can't enforce. A corollary to the latter
might be: Never give an order you don't intend to follow up to see
that it gets done.

Cases in point are many. They range from the obvious to the
obscure. The Army haircut policy is very clear. There are pictures
to illustrate it. Yet there is grousing by senior officer and NCOs
about the unkempt appearance of some of our soldiers. The solution is obvious. At morning inspections, squad leaders and section
chiefs should be checking their men. Staff officers and NCOs
should be doing likewise.

That problem, the haircut issue, is relatively insignificant.
What is far more important is the compliance with orders in combat. If a battalion has not followed the brigade order for a given
operation, that lapse could very well endanger the success of the
mission and the lives of countless men in other units. The failure
of the field artillery to deliver fires precisely when and where called
for is another mortal sin in combat.

A commander must constantly check to see that, in the first
place, his orders are clear and have been understood; then he must
check to see to it they are being carried out. This is true of maintenance, supply, administration, pay (one of the most important
things that a commander can check for his troops), and the mess.
In combat, the commander is constantly checking the conduct of
the battle, stationing himself where he is in the best position to
influence the action, to commit his reserves, to call for additional
fire when and where needed, and to accomplish his mission.

In normal, day-to-day peacetime activities, the wise commander, staff officer, or NCO has some sort of a tickler file to permit him to follow up on projects on a timely basis. One arrangement is to put a tickler in a suspense file so that on a certain date the tickler arrives back on your desk to remind you to check. Still another method is a simple three-by-five card file with notes on various projects alphabetically arranged for easy reference. Three-by-five cards can also be used as a sort of poor man's data bank for information to which one refers constantly.

No matter the system (and one's brain, unaided, is rarely responsive enough to do the job) the rule is simplicity itself: Personally follow up those things you want done well.

Humility, like cleanliness, is next to Godliness.

Humility

How often one sees arrogance attempt to cover up incompetence, bullishness camouflage insecurity, and impatience mask indecisiveness. Such symptoms could be readily overcome with some minor injections of humility.

A humble man is not necessarily a Milquetoast. A humble man is, however, one who does not take all the credit himself for his unit's accomplishments. He does not hog the show. He is not afraid to give credit where credit is due. A humble man is generally a self-confident one who knows his own capabilities. He is also not afraid to take the rap for his unit's failings and to admit that he made a mistake. "I blew that one" is good for the soul and the psyche.

One of the least arrogant and least conceited men I knew became Chief of Staff of the U.S. Army—Gen. Creighton W. Abrams. He knew his strengths and his shortcomings. He was not afraid to give credit. He was not afraid to ask questions. (He's the man who said that the only dumb question was the one that did not get asked.) He was not afraid to poke fun at himself occasionally. Once, when he walked into a conference room filled with generals, a loud-voiced lieutenant colonel intoned stentoriously: "Gentlemen, the Chief of Staff." The Chief looked a bit embarrassed and then said, "Okay, but where in the hell are the trumpets?"

He was not an egotistic man. He knew that he got to be Chief of Staff by hard work, logical thought processes, and the ability to get a job done in peace and in war. He was perfectly willing to admit his mistakes even to congressional committees. When asked by a congressman to describe the utility of the .45-caliber pistol, he said that it was "great for defending oneself in a crowded elevator." And he was not above delivering newspapers on a cold Sunday morning to the NCO barracks at Fort Myer, Virginia, when the regular newsboy, his son, was ill and could not make the rounds. His only grousing was directed at the other generals at Fort Myer who did not get out to shovel the snow off their sidewalks. Long before Congress started hacking away at the large cars used by senior government officials, this Chief of Staff had traded in his limousine for a compact sedan. And on many cold, dark mornings at Fort Myer, the Chief, after walking around the post for exercise, would stop in an EM mess hall for a cup of coffee with the troops.

Sgt. Maj. Carlos Leal was one of the finest NCOs I ever knew; he was also a superb man, a great husband, and a devoted and understanding father. He was so well-grounded in things military that he could tell in very short order how a unit or another NCO was performing. He was a perfectionist. He turned up often in the most unexpected places and situations to see for himself what was going on. His surprise visits as the post and division sergeant major at Fort Riley immeasurably bucked up operations across the board. But Carlos was not haughty, overbearing, or filled with his own self-importance. He was a humble man who knew what high standards were and saw to it that they were met. Humility is far from indifference.

How does humility fit into command? How does humility affect leadership? The humble man is aware of his own shortcomings and does not seek to hide them within an aura of bluster or behind a screen of impatience. The humble leader knows that his staff and subordinates are smart, too, and have valid and worthwhile ideas from time to time. The humble man at least lends an ear to his staff and his troops; then he makes his decision.

Humility coupled with competence, self-confidence, and full knowledge of one's own capabilities and limitations are the ingredients that make an outstanding commander and top-notch person.

Informing the Troops

The matter of keeping the troops informed is very controversial. On the one hand, it is perfectly clear that well-informed troops who believe in their mission, who believe that what they are doing is right and proper, will sacrifice their comfort—and their lives, if necessary—to accomplish their mission. On the other hand, it is also perfectly clear that a commander cannot always explain in detail what it is his unit is going to do; he may lack the time or opportunity, or it may be classified. At best, the troops know what is expected of them and have a sincere belief that that is what is best for them. At worst, a unit will debate, argue, discuss endlessly whether or not a given course of action is good for them (see Rap Sessions).

Obviously, in peacetime, in a garrison situation, it is far easier to keep the troops informed than it is in combat. In peacetime, a commander, depending on his level, has many devices for informing the troops and their dependents. One used by senior commanders is a weekly column in the local post newspaper in which he discusses topics of immediate interest (see Commander's Comments—not to be confused with the Chaplain's Corner-type of discussion).

The company or battery commander has a perfect opportunity to keep the troops informed at Morning Parade. In that program there is a time set aside each day specifically for the commander to talk to his men and let them know what is going on. This is the best and most convenient way for commanders to keep the troops abreast.

Daily bulletins are only marginally useful for putting out information, because they are so uniformly unread by the troops that no one can be certain that a very large portion of the unit ever gets around to reading it.

103

Bulletin boards can also be used to get out the message—but not always. Cartoonists lampooning the military life often show the "Sad Sack" rummaging through the items on a bulletin board and finding at the bottom G. Washington's order for crossing the Delaware.

Direct contact with individual men or small groups is most effective in getting the word out. Another very effective way to inform the troops is at unit functions where the CO presents an award or singles out an individual or sub-unit for praise (see Credit). At such a formation, the CO can give a short speech to emphasize a point he wishes to get across.

The worst way to inform the troops is by rumor, half-baked reports, wives' club small talk, happy hour conversations, or other rumor mills. Gossip does nothing but create unrest, misery, and unhappiness. (One dependent in Germany at the time of the Berlin crisis hanged herself when she heard an incorrect rumor that all dependents were to be evacuated.) The commander must himself be properly informed, and then he must put out the word directly, clearly, and as soon as possible.

Generally speaking, the troops have a right to know what is going on and how various events affect them, their lives, and their families. And within reason, every commander must keep his men up to date. But a commander must not mislead his men; he must level with them; he must make every effort to do what he says he is going to do; and in this connection, it is usually better to report that something has already been accomplished (a new snack bar, a new club, a new training program) than to talk about obscure, unprogrammed plans and possibilities for the vague future. The new barracks four years down the road has relatively little interest for troops who are still living in World War II barracks.

One device that a battalion commander found very useful was what he called his "Game Plan." He listed under three headings Administration, Training, and Operations in simple terms what his policies and goals were and what specifically he expected from his outfit. Then he held a conference with all of his commanders and first sergeants and explained the details of the chart. He distributed copies to each of them. He directed the company commanders to hold a similar meeting with their troops, explain the chart, and post it locally on the bulletin board. Obviously, such a system can be used only for an overall plan, cannot be used very often, and even at best cannot be expected to get to all of the troops. But it is one way to get the word out.

So far, I've been speaking mostly about administrative, peacetime information and the dissemination thereof. Battle plans and briefings are entirely different matters. They cannot be left to chance or happenstance. They must be thorough and reach each man.

One of the best-briefed and most carefully rehearsed combat operations that I know about was the Son Tay Raid by about 110 Green Berets and Rangers into North Vietnam to rescue the POWs allegedly imprisoned at Son Tay. Because 90 percent of the men involved in the raid were from my command (the JFK Center for Special Warfare), I was privy to the preparations. The late Col. "Bull" Simon, a master of unconventional warfare and ground commander of the raid, took the men to Eglin Air Force Base in Florida, where they were isolated in a remote section of the base. One of the items used for briefing the troops was a scale model of the Son Tay camp developed by another government agency. The model was so detailed and accurate that by dimming the lights in the room and using a special viewing lens, one would get the feel of what the camp would look like in limited light at night.

In another area at Eglin there was a full-blown model of the camp, but it was not nearly as detailed as the scale model. The full-blown camp was accurate in dimension and in the principal facilities, however. The plan for the raid was rehearsed time and again on the full-scale model; each man knew exactly where his helicopter would land, precisely what he was to do, and who would be with him; he knew the alternate plans as well as the principal one; by raid time, he could accomplish his mission in the dark—which is what he did. The result of all this preparation was a very hollow success: The raid was executed with clocklike precision, but unfortunately, the POWs had been moved. Nonetheless, the Son Tay raid is exemplary of how to prepare for and conduct such an operation.

Informing and rehearsing the troops can run the gamut from the Son Tay model to the squad leader orienting his troops by using a stick and a map sketched in the dirt. But no matter how it is done, briefing and informing the troops before a combat mission is so essential that its necessity almost goes without saying.

So, in short, keep the troops informed when at all possible; but once the plan is made, the decision adopted, stick with it—the time for debate and decision is over.

You can't have it both ways.

Inspections

Ever since the Vietnam era, our abolition of the draft, our initiation of the Volunteer Army, it seems that we have developed an inherent fear of inspections, that we are violating a man's rights if we look critically at his barracks and living area, if we conduct surprise command maintenance inspections, if we insist upon detailed inspection of the men in ranks. We have sometimes even gone so far as to forbid maintenance inspections and instead conduct "maintenance assistance visits" by our so-called maintenance experts.

As far as barracks' appearance goes, I am firmly convinced that if we do not inspect barracks on a daily basis, they will shortly become slums. And if we do not inspect the troops in ranks, they too will become raunchy, unkempt, and unmilitary. Well, one might say, so what? What difference does it make, as long as they do their jobs? Why this great emphasis on correct and trim personal appearance and orderly and clean barracks?

I, for one, believe that a soldier should look like a soldier, and that he should be a model of neatness in his barracks, his dress, and his grooming. The military profession is a way of life, proud, tradition-filled, and of utmost necessity in our world. (We've needed armies almost since Adam and Eve had the first fight and were summarily banished from Paradise to initiate a human race of less than angelic persuasions.) The military profession is vital to the life of our country and our way of life. Therefore, it must be as perfect as we can make it. Do inspections lead to perfection? Certainly.

Industries have quality control; the Army has inspections. Without them, we would have no idea of how we are doing, of how our supplies are being managed and used, of how our administration is being handled, of how our vehicles are being maintained, of how ready our units are for combat. A leader who does not inspect his men, their weapons, their orders, their understanding of their mission before a combat operation, is guilty of malpractice and negligence of the first order.

A unit that is proud of itself, that knows that it is good, that knows that it does things properly, whose commander conducts routine inspections, is never afraid of or unprepared for an inspection from higher headquarters. In fact, it is proud to show itself off. This is the ultimate.

Sometimes inspections can go pretty far toward the other end of the spectrum from "just a cursory look." I remember one command inspection that was spit and polish all the way. After we had returned to Japan from Korea in the fall of 1953, the regimental combat team commander told me that he would conduct a command inspection of my battalion, to include full field layout and all men in ranks.

The preparation for such a command inspection consumed the full time of all men for days. By the day of inspection we were blitzed, polished, painted, and ready. The inspection went like this: Behind the rows of pup tents, the vehicles and artillery pieces were lined up. All mess equipment was laid out. As a matter of fact, the entire TO and E of my parachute artillery battalion was on display. We lined up the tent poles of the men's pup tents with an aiming circle. For the individual displays of equipment in front of each tent, each man wrapped his underclothes around pieces of cardboard the same size. Each man in each battery had toothbrushes, not only of the same brand, but also of the same color. Ditto for shaving cream, razors, and blades. The vehicles were displayed with the hoods up. The drivers had shined the spark plugs and the copper tubing with blitz cloths. The engines were immaculately clean. The bodies of the vehicles had been simonized. Black rubber paint polished the tires. The howitzers had been repainted and waxed to perfection. Shovels, entrenching tools, pickaxes had been sanded and/or painted. The field mess equipment had been shined with steel wool until it glistened. The men themselves were in spit-shined jump boots, their belt buckles polished on *both* sides, and the khakis they wore had never been sat in. Their brass shone in the morning sun. It was a sparkling display.

Such an inspection had many faults and abuses—although it

was not all bad. It was a throwback to the pre–World War II Army in which every man had two sets of field equipment—one for wear and one for display. But such an inspection only partially revealed the true serviceability of the equipment. As a matter of fact, after that inspection (for which we received high accolades from the CO and his staff), I told the motor officer that blitzed spark plugs were a thing of the past—now we were going to concentrate on making all the vehicles run.

But there is a happy medium. When men live as close to one another as they do in the Army, we must pay attention to them and inspect them and their equipment. When we are entrusted with millions of dollars' worth of equipment, we must not only be accountable for it, we must ensure that it is in top-notch condition. And the only way to do that is to inspect it.

There is absolutely no need to fear inspections, be they from the IG, the Army Audit Agency, or the congressional watchdogs, the General Accounting Office. The solution is to be ready all the time. And to be ready all the time requires constant checking. A company commander should inspect all areas of his company on a daily basis. Squad leaders should inspect their men daily. Battalion commanders should cover all parts of their battalions thoroughly each week. These checks are for neatness, orderliness, and condition of equipment and facilities. Commanders and NCOs check for leaky showers, broken windows, clogged drains, burned-out lights, and inadequate police. But they should also be looking at the way the men are doing their jobs in the motor pool, the mess, and supply room, the orderly room. It doesn't take a management genius to determine if men are following proper, logical, and efficient procedures. In the motor pool, if men have to walk back and forth from the toolbox to the vehicle they're repairing, it's simple enough to move the toolbox.

A command maintenance inspection that looks at all aspects of a maintenance operation is good because it forces the unit into proper procedures and practices. So are annual general inspections. (Maintenance assistance visits are fine once or twice; but until you *inspect* the unit, you're not going to be sure that the unit is implementing the proper procedures. Assistance visits are no substitutes for inspections.)

Preparing for command maintenance inspections and annual

general inspections bucks up a unit considerably. A unit with haphazard maintenance policies, no inspections of barracks, messes, supply rooms, orderly rooms, or of men in ranks is bound to be unkempt, slovenly, unmilitary, and therefore, not combat-ready. The Russian Army after the Revolution, wherein all men were theoretically equal and officers wore no rank, is a perfect example of how a military force can disintegrate without high standards of discipline. History is replete with similar illustrations of military forces crumbling into worthlessness through lack of command and control.

It's impossible to have a slovenly, neglected, combat-ready outfit. The terms are mutually exclusive.

Inspections

The ultimate virtue.

Integrity

In these troubled times, with our institutions from the highest level of government to churches, schools, businesses, and sports riddled by scandals, the Army leader, traditionally a model of incorruptibility, must examine himself, his motives, his goals, his desires, and his code of conduct. If he finds himself wanting in integrity, he is useless to the Army in peace or in war. Integrity is the fundamental principle on which an officer, commissioned or noncommissioned, builds his whole being. Of the three basic precepts of the West Point motto—Duty, Honor, Country—Honor is the most important because without it the others are meaningless and hollow.

A former Chief of Staff of the Army, Gen. W. C. Westmoreland, felt so strongly about the necessity for integrity in the officer corps that he sent the following message to each officer in the Army:

To the Officers of the Army:

I want to make it clear beyond any question that absolute integrity of an officer's word, deed, and signature is a matter that permits no compromise. Inevitably, in the turmoil of the times, every officer will be confronted by situations which test his character. On these occasions he must stand on his principles, for these are the crucial episodes that determine the worth of a man.

While basic laws underlie command authority, the real foundation of successful leadership is the moral authority derived from professional competence and integrity. Competence and integrity are not separable. The officer who sacrifices his integrity sacrifices all; he will lose the respect and trust of those he seeks to lead, and he will degrade the reputation of his profession. The good repute of the officer corps is a responsibility shared by every officer. Each

111

one of us stands in the light of his brother, and each shares in the honor and burden of leadership. Dedicated and selfless service to our country is our primary motivation. This makes our profession a way of life rather than just a job.

My endorsement to that message to the officers of my command (the 1st Inf. Div.) was as follows:

1. Bring the attached message from the Chief of Staff to the attention of all officers in your command. Make it clear that adherence to these principles is mandatory—without qualification, compromise, or equivocation.

2. Above all other traits of character or personality, an officer must first have integrity and honesty in all of his actions and decisions. And the just and fair treatment of soldiers entrusted to his care are parts of integrity. We can excuse a young officer initially for not knowing his job or for lack of experience; we can never excuse or condone his dishonesty, injustice toward his men, or a display of a lack of integrity.

3. I expect each officer in this command to understand and govern himself according to the precepts which the Chief of Staff has clearly dictated. I expect each commander in the chain of command to judge himself and his subordinates according to these principles, to establish them as standards of conduct, and to accept no deviation therefrom.

What really is integrity? A dictionary defines it as "rigid adherence to a code of behavior, probity." And probity? "Complete and confirmed integrity, uprightness." And in each case the dictionary further defines integrity and probity "see synonyms at *honesty*." Thus, integrity is a constant; it is not a sometime thing. It is rigid, complete, and unwavering. It brooks no deviation from honorable conduct. It requires total honesty in all things at all times. A West Point cadet lives constantly within the commandment and is imbued with the motto that he not "lie, cheat, or steal." An officer's signature, his word, his handshake is his honor.

In no profession is integrity more important than in the profession of arms because in no other profession are so many men's lives at stake. No other profession bears the weight of the security of the nation. No other profession calls upon men to make life and death decisions for other men. Therefore, in no other profession are integrity, probity, and honesty so important. If an officer or an NCO does not have integrity as his bond, his foundation, his core, no matter what else he has, he's a failure. There is no place for him in the military establishment.

Give a man a job to do and then let him do it.

Jobs

Often we have heard the above dictum. But how seldom we put it into practice. As leaders, we tend to overcontrol because we fear that the shortcomings of one of our subordinates will reflect unfavorably upon us. We get in the habit of assigning officers instead of NCOs to supervise various operations that are clearly NCO jobs and responsibilities (often by direction of some insecure commander up the line). The NCOs could, in fact, probably do a much better job (because of greater pertinent experience) if given the responsibility. We fall into the habit of telling our men precisely how to do a given job or accomplish a given mission.

To build self-confidence in our junior leaders, to let them learn by doing, we must give them their heads. This does not contradict the need for inspections. Rather we should give a man a job, a time for completion, the wherewithal to do it, and then let him get on with it.

One example among many comes to mind. In Korea, I was the Deputy Eighth Army CG in 1974. We needed a barracks built for an MP platoon that was the guard unit for a new stockade. The Engineer Battalion CO and I selected a lieutenant and his platoon of engineers, gave him the mission, and left him alone. Precisely on time, within the funds allotted, the young man and his platoon were finished. They were proud troops when they turned the building over to the MP detachment.

The same principle holds for combat operations. Give a man a mission, see to it he has the power to accomplish it, and then turn him loose. Check him occasionally to see if he needs help; interfere if a disaster is pending; but generally, let the commander command.

During the Vietnam War, the helicopter and our all-encompass-ing, pervasive communications network made commanders so omnipresent that sometimes they suffocated their subordinates. Many senior commanders could and did overcontrol their junior leaders. I remember flying with a division commander over a battalion operations area. He circled the operation and, using the superb radios in his helicopter, almost ran the battle going on below. His comments were pithy, arrogant, and detailed. It was a perfect example of overcontrol and must have frustrated and discouraged the battalion CO on the ground.

Another raconteur said that "good judgment comes from experience; experience comes from bad judgment."

Let the commanders command, check occasionally, bail their subordinates if a debacle is about to engulf them; but in general, give a man a job and then let him do it.

Fire control computer. U.S. Army photo

Learn another.

Language

In the military service, we spend perhaps a third of our careers in overseas assignments. Yet for the most part, unless we are assigned to specialized programs such as military attachés or military assistance programs, we make no effort to learn the language of the country. This is a grave mistake. (Admittedly, certain bon vivants very quickly learn the proper phrase in any language from Amharic to Zūnian in order to strike up friendships of one kind or another with the *frauleins, femmes,* and *tomodachis,* in whatever country they may find themselves. This is not exactly what I had in mind.)

One of the foremost linguists in the Army, and at one point its highest ranking member, was Gen. Maxwell Taylor. When he arrived in Korea to take over the United Nations Command, he gave his arrival speech in both English and Hangul, the language of Korea. He spoke other languages fluently. Obviously, he had a knack for languages, but he worked at it. (As Chief of Staff of the Army, he kept a German phrase book in his bathroom at the Pentagon in anticipation of a trip to Germany he was about to make. Obviously, he also made every minute count.)

Another high-ranking officer who had a flair for languages was Lt. Gen. Vernon Walters. His career was a succession of assignments wherein he had to use foreign languages. He was an interpreter for President Eisenhower in French and German. But he also spoke Russian, Italian, and other languages fluently. He finished his career as deputy director of the CIA and is now a roving ambassador for the secretary of state.

Central Army Group (CENTAG) in Germany was formerly composed of Americans, French, and Germans. (The French no longer play a very large role in CENTAG.) However, a few years ago, the G-2, in anticipation of a visit to CENTAG by the Korean ambassador to France, went to the post library, took out a Korean

116

language record, memorized a few phrases in Hangul, and the next day astounded and pleased the CENTAG commander by greeting his guest, the Korean ambassador, in Hangul. The G-2 then proceeded to brief them in French, in which the Ambassador was fluent. The ambassador was impressed that the briefer had taken the trouble to learn at least a few words in his language, however he may have massacred them, and CENTAG won another friend. That same G-2 had the confidence and will to brief twenty French generals in French and even took their questions in their own language. The least that could be said for him was that he was brave. He also learned enough German to give a five-minute introduction to a briefing for some visiting German generals.

In Vietnam, a knowledge of French was obviously of great help when dealing with the senior Vietnamese officers. Many of them spoke French fluently, but not English. Therefore, in dealing with them, it was much simpler to speak French than to try to converse laboriously through interpreters.

One of my more interesting moments in Vietnam came when I was a special assistant to COMUSMACV. I was also his liaison officer to the Chairman of the Vietnamese JGS, Gen. Cao Van Vien. One day General Vien called me into his office and told me, in English which he spoke quite fluently, that he was scheduled to brief President Johnson on Guam in the very near future and he wanted me to write the briefing for him. Then General Vien said: "And so that you will understand exactly what I want to say in the briefing to the president, I am now going to speak French." The rust shook off my French very rapidly because there was no one else in the office to help me. (And it is also not true that that's why the North Vietnamese won the war.)

Languages are not difficult to learn, especially the spoken language, and particularly when one is stationed in a foreign country. There are always tutors and classes available and, obviously, many natives on whom to practice. All it takes is ambition and time.

The rewards are great. Americans have a reputation in foreign countries of being enclave-bound, aloof, detached, and seemingly superior to the local gentry. By learning a few phrases of greeting in the local tongue, one is able to break the ice and help to change a foreigner's view of the miscalled Ugly American.

No matter what the country, the officials and the people thereof are flattered if visitors—especially Americans—take the time to learn a few words of their language. But more than that, an American officer or NCO should learn at least one other language fluently and keep up his fluency throughout his career. For many officers and NCOs in the past, it has meant some excellent assignments that otherwise would not have been available. Simultaneously with his own, such an officer or NCO enhances the reputation of the U.S. Army in foreign countries.

Learn another language

Remember—it can be learned.

Leadership

This whole book is about leadership; nonetheless, this chapter provides an opportunity to emphasize a lot of what has been said about leadership by hundreds of leaders. Here's my own definition: To be a superior leader, one must be hard but fair and compassionate.

Be hard: Set high standards and insist that they be met. Know your own job and where you fit into the system and insist that your subordinates do also. Require that correct procedures be followed in whatever pursuit you are directing. Use your men in the MOS's for which they have been trained. When you give an order, insist that it be carried out. Set high standards of discipline. Require soldiers to soldier. Don't compromise integrity.

But fair: Never give an order that cannot be carried out. Give a man a job and let him do it. Let a man make mistakes as he learns. Consult with your men (but don't take votes—the Army is not a democracy). Use the chain of command. Assign missions by unit, whether it be simple details or combat missions. Put the regular unit leader in charge. Reward exceptional performance in public; correct and chew out inferior or slovenly performance in private. Make the punishment fit the crime. Make sure your men know how they are doing and that you pass on compliments from outside and higher headquarters. Make the individual responsible for a well-defined, self-contained piece of the action (called participative management by the management types).

With compassion: Know your men, their needs and their problems. Try to solve them. Listen. Take care of your men and be loyal to them. Shield them from harassment from higher headquarters. Train them for their jobs. Give them leave when they want it if at all possible. (Leave is a right, not a privilege.) Make certain that their pay is straight (this is also a right). *Listen to both sides of every story.* (That may be one of the most important precepts in this chapter.) Don't haze the troops, but make certain that they are in the highest state of physical condition (this is for their own good and is thus a measure of compassion). Respect their time off even though a soldier is a soldier twenty-four hours a day. Teach him and train him to survive in combat. And never punish an entire unit for the transgressions of an unknown few; find the culprits and punish them.

Above all else, remember this: Leadership is not necessarily something one is born with—it can definitely be learned.

> A leader is best when he is neither seen nor heard.
> Not so good when he is adored and glorified.
> Worst when he is hated and despised.
> "Fail to honor people, they will fail to honor you";
> But of a good leader, who talks little, his aim fulfilled,
> They will say, "We did this ourselves."
>
> Lao-tse

The postman rings many times.

Letters

In today's Army, the company commander is snowed under with mail. He must answer congressional inquiries, letters from parents whose sons do not write them, letters from troops' creditors, letters from higher headquarters, letters from distraught wives, letters from jilted fiancées (often in another country), letters from his men in the stockade (now, I believe, called a correction facility, or some such), and letters from a wide variety of other sources. And he must also initiate letters. He sends out letters of recommendation, letters of reprimand, and letters of inquiry.

The worst example of a letter from a company commander was one sent by a young commander in an overseas area who was attempting to curb the VD rate in his company. This misguided young man made it his policy to send letters to the wives of his soldiers informing the wives that their husbands had contracted VD and that they ought to know about it. He thought, erroneously, that the wives would put pressure on their husbands to cease and desist from such untoward behavior. What the young man caused instead was a near mutiny on the part of his troops. Such a solution to the VD problem is thoughtless, disloyal, and apt to instigate divorce proceedings in a number of homes along with a contract on the head of the writer.

The problem of letter proliferation suggests a few rules:

1. When writing to the wife or mother of a soldier who has done a good job, specify just what it is that he has been doing very well.

2. Answer mail promptly even if with an interim reply that simply acknowledges receipt of the original inquiry; follow up with a letter based on the facts.

3. Avoid making promises.

4. Be brief, factual, and to the point.

5. Send only the original letter; there is nothing more wasteful than sending an original and two or three copies of letters.

6. If you have no typist, write the letter in longhand.

Letter writing is a very personal thing. You, the writer—the company commander, the battalion commander, even the platoon leader or platoon sergeant—are putting yourself in the position of making a statement to or about one of your men or women that will be read with great interest, because the letter supposedly is in reply to something that has been bothering that soldier or his family. Form letters just do not fill the bill; nor do letters written in the name of the CO about important matters. And no matter how trivial the subject may seem to you, it is extremely important to the writer.

And so it seems appropriate to quote again one of the most quotable of our Chiefs of Staff, General Abrams. He said: "By people I do not mean 'personnel.' I do not mean 'end-strength.' I do not mean 'percent of fill,' or any of these other labels which refer to people as a commodity. They have needs and interests and desires. They have spirit, and will, and strengths, and abilities. They have weaknesses and faults. And they have names."

If you remember and practice that bit of philosophy, you'll have no trouble putting "compassion" into your leadership and your letter writing.

Try me first.

Letters to the CO

One division commander (me), an ardent nonbeliever in the so-called open-door policy, devised a system whereby allegedly aggrieved troops could have access to him. It was simply this: He invited his soldiers and their dependents to write him a letter stating the problem, complaint, question, or suggestion. The commander published his offer in the post newspaper with a view toward cutting down on Congressionals, making himself accessible to the troops (and their dependents), and unearthing the problems within his division.

In a period of some twenty-two months the division commander received 2,366 letters. With such a volume, and knowing that each letter contained a problem that had to be solved, the commander replied to each letter the day he received it. It was admittedly a form letter (but individually typed and personally signed by the CG) and said that, in effect, the man's letter had been received, the commander was studying it, and the writer would hear from the commander in a few days. Then in three or four days, the commander wrote again to the writer telling him what had been done about his case. Naturally, such a system required a follow-up suspense file, a lot of staff work, and an education of the staff that the commander meant business and that the troops and their dependents' problems would be solved.

The statistics on the mail are rather interesting. Of the total letters written, 2,127 were legitimate complaints. The gripes ran the gamut from requests to speed up elimination from the service to requests to be allowed to remain in the service. (Admittedly, a great many of the writers were men in the stockade who wanted a quick discharge, no matter what kind. Another large group of writers were men who had been picked up as deserters and were

123

being processed through the installation for discharge or other disposition.) Additional areas of concern were pay and other financial problems (especially since this was the period when the Army was shifting over to the automated JUMPS pay system which had many bugs in the beginning), disciplinary woes (punishment too severe or unjust), nonsupport (from wives, many of these were sad, heartrending stories), medical problems, compassionate reassignments, re-enlistments, housing. Surprisingly, even though the division had a very stringent haircut policy, there were only one or two letters from men who complained about that policy.

The Letters to the CO program had many beneficial effects. In the first place, the commander was able to assist 2,246 of the writers. And certainly in those cases that could not be helped, the knowledge that the division CG was interested enough to write and explain the circumstances was at least a boost to morale.

But perhaps the biggest beneficiary of the program was the staff. Naturally, each letter had to be staffed to learn both sides of the story and to solve the problem. Since there were many problems repeatedly reported, the solution to one man's problem and the resultant correction of a deficient staff procedure automatically solved that problem for a number of men. It thus improved staff procedures, and since the staff was aware that the commander had a suspense date on each of the actions, it speeded up the procedures.

Another beneficiary was the command chain down the line. Commanders at the company level naturally were involved when one of their men wrote to the division commander. The company commander had to look into both sides of the situation, which caused him to be alert to problems so that his men would have no need to write to the division commander.

Wives, mothers, and girlfriends who wrote to the commander learned that he had a heart and that he was interested in the welfare of his men and their dependents.

And finally, the whole division and the post benefited because a good many of the suggestions were implemented for the benefit of all the troops and families on the post.

Admittedly, such a system violates to some degree the use of the chain of command. But once the system is in place and working for a time, the chain of command begins to function, and the Letters to the CO program gradually phases itself out. That's the ultimate goal.

A battalion commander might very well initiate the same procedure, and he can expect the same beneficial results—on a lesser scale, of course—that the division commander experienced. His staff would also be educated to problems and feel compelled to get on with their solutions. His company commanders would become aware of their problems. It's a tricky procedure but, properly used, can be a great success.

Loyalty

We talk often about loyalty to one's organization, to one's business firm, to one's ideals and beliefs, and to one's country. This is all well and good. But there is another side to the coin of loyalty: loyalty down the chain to one's men.

Loyalty "down" should not be confused with permissiveness, vote-gathering, or popularity contests. Downward loyalty is far different. It means that a commander (or a boss or a supervisor) will stand up for his men when they are in difficulty, will listen to their problems when they are troubled, and will see to it that injustices are righted when they are wronged.

But there is another important part as it pertains to the Army. A commander is bound to protect his men and to see to it that they are not needlessly exposed to injury and/or death in training or in combat. Thus, in training, the commander must ensure that his men have the kind of rugged training and discipline that will permit survival and success in combat. It takes a strong commander to insist on this kind of training and discipline.

A Jane Fonda or a member of the American Civil Liberties Union might see what I have just said as a rationalization designed to permit a commander to demand rugged training and harsh discipline in the name of loyalty to one's men and/or cover up a streak of sadism. In spite of Jane Fonda's time spent with the North Vietnamese in Hanoi during the late debacle, I doubt that she has led too many men (or women, for that matter) in combat. And I suspect that the ACLU ranks are not filled with very many members eligible for membership in the American Legion.

Loyalty to one's troops demands that we train them and discipline them precisely so that they will be effective in combat and the fewest possible will be killed or wounded. That is a heavy burden of responsibility that every commander takes upon himself when he dons the green tabs of a commander.

After World War II, the mighty U.S. WW II war machine disintegrated. The part of the U.S. Army occupying Japan became soft, inadequate, and combat unworthy. In *This Kind of War*, a book about the Japan Occupation Force's unpreparedness for fighting at the beginning of the Korean War, T. R. Fehrenbach* makes this statement:

> There is no place left to go, and all across the thin Perimeter Line American soldiers are stiffening. Hatred for the enemy was beginning to sear them, burning through their earlier indifference to the war. And everywhere, the first disastrous shock of combat was wearing off. Beaten and bloody from the hard lessons of war, troops were beginning to listen to their officers, heed what their older sergeants told them.
>
> A man who has seen and smelled his first corpse on the battlefield soon loses his preconceived notions of what the soldier's trade is all about. He learns how it is in combat, and how it must always be. He becomes a soldier, or he dies.
>
> The men of the 1st Cavalry, the 2nd, 24th, and 25th Divisions in Korea were becoming soldiers. For underneath the misconceptions of their society, the softness and mawkishness, the human material was hard and good.
>
> There have been many brave men in the ranks, but they were learning that bravery by itelf has little to do with success in battle. On line, most normal men are afraid, have been afraid, or will be afraid. Only when disciplined to obey orders quickly and willingly, can such fear be controlled. Only when superbly trained and conditioned against the shattering experience of war, only knowing almost from rote what to do, can men carry out their tasks come what may. And knowing they are disciplined, trained, and conditioned brings pride to men—pride in their own toughness, their own ability; and this pride will hold them true when all else fails.

That eloquent extract summarizes millions of words that have been written and spoken about the need for training and discipline and combat-readiness for our military forces. And it lays on commanders a weighty requirement: loyalty to their troops, which equates with requirements for readiness.

*T.R. Fehrenbach, *This Kind of War* (New York: Macmillan, 1963).

There is still another side to loyalty, which often gets mixed up with a lot of other emotions: This is loyalty that requires a man to stand up and be counted. This facet of loyalty is especially important for staff officers who think that their bosses are going off in the wrong direction or are about to make a bad decision. It is the duty of the subordinate to advise his boss of what he thinks. Then, if the boss decides to continue on, at least the staff officer has made an honest attempt to right what he considers to be a wrong. And once the boss has made the decision, the subordinate must try to carry it out.

This involves a lot of other problems, however. If the decision is clearly immoral, against regulations, severely detrimental to the command, the subordinate has a few options left. He can reopen the case with his boss; he can take the situation to the inspector general; he can go over his boss's head to the next higher headquarters (a very risky business—the subordinate had better be right); he can ask for relief (witness the action of Attorney General Richardson when he was asked to fire the Watergate prosecutor). I certainly do not recommend that the subordinate write his congressman; there are better ways to solve a problem.

One incident involving loyalty comes to mind. When I was commanding the 674th Parachute Field Artillery Battalion in Japan after the Korean War, I had attached to my battalion the AAA battery of the regimental combat team. The AAA battery commander was a very strong-willed, opinionated, hard-nosed officer who had a bit of a chip on his shoulder because of his AAA small-gun status amid a bunch of proud, airborne tube-artillerymen. At a battery commanders' call one day, after I had said that I wanted accurate reveille formation reports, the AAA battery commander asked me, courteously enough, how he was supposed to do that in the dark at reveille. I explained, admittedly a bit sarcastically, that you take a report by having the squad leader check his squad, report to the platoon sergeant, who reports to the first sergeant, who reports to the B.C.

The AAA battery commander was embarrassed by my comments and, thereafter, was proper but very cold in his relationship to me personally. A couple of days later, I called him in to my office and, after he reported very formally, I said, "Bob, what's your problem?'' He said, "Sir, I can never be loyal to you.'' I said, "Captain, sit down. You and I have a lot to talk about.''

After a long discussion, in which he finally told me of his embarrassment at my comments about how to take a report, and after I admitted that I had been wrong in singling him out with a touch of sarcasm, we parted on a new note of understanding. And, thereafter, in that battalion, in matters social and official, he became one of my most ardent supporters.

Loyalty obviously travels a two-way street—it goes down as well as up.

Keep the troops informed. U.S. Army photo

Patton's Law: "A good plan today is better than a perfect plan tomorrow."

Management

The high gurus of management have written millions of words about how best to utilize resources in accomplishing a job; hundreds of seminars are conducted daily to spread this or that management discipline or new theory; learned management savants drill executives in all kinds of gimmicky systems, principles, plans, and processes for how best to accomplish their tasks. All these management expositions presumably have one goal: to teach managers how to accomplish tasks—which one must assume are necessary—with fewer men, in less time, and with fewer materials. (Put another way: How to increase productivity without adding men, time, or other resources or, simply, how to get things done.)

No matter what we call it, a good leader ("manager" in civilian jargon) must know where he is going and how he is going to get there; he must plot his course and then, by regular reviews of the situation, see to it that he remains on course. If he veers from his objective or goal, whether it is the next hill in combat or the successful completion of an inspection or the development of the Vietnamese National Defense College, he must take the necessary actions to get himself and his unit back on the track and on the timetable to arrive at the required place at the required time. Squad leaders must do it and so must the Commander in Chief.

At the lowest level of management (or leadership)—at the gun crew, the squad, the fire-team level—the leader checks every detail and follows every action along the way to assure success. But as the level of responsibility increases, the techniques become a little different, until at the very top, the leader is managing by exception: He gets involved only when the program gets off the track.

In simplest terms, any manager can solve a problem by taking these steps: He sets his goal or objective; he breaks the job down into manageable tasks; he assigns each task to a subordinate or unit; he spells out clearly what he wants and by when he wants it done; he coordinates all parts so that the entire project is finished simultaneously at the assigned time; then he checks periodically (but not so often that he is interfering) to see that his subordinates are on schedule.

To avoid the pitfalls of the bureaucrat, the good manager takes a few simple precautions. Among them might be the following:

1. Consolidate, eliminate, reduce structure of staff and organization.

2. Decrease the layering of his staffs (for example, there is no need for a deputy in a staff section of three officers).

3. Eliminate unnecessary functions.

4. Reduce administration, reports, paperwork.

5. Use the chain of command.

6. Eliminate boards, committees, councils, other crutches.

7. Take the administrative load off the busy levels (the company, battery and troop levels) and centralize it at the battalion or higher. (One ingenious recent development is the removal of typewriters from the company level; but I suspect that many company commanders and first sergeants have acquired their own through purchase or barter.)

8. Decentralize actions to the lowest level possible. (It's always been a mystery to me that an action officer, say a lieutenant colonel, on a high-level staff, making a visit to a "field" installation evidences so much more intelligence than the major general commanding that installation.)

9. Have faith in your subordinates.

By whatever names they go these days, these rules should help to get a job done efficiently, cheaply, and speedily.

The following quote is perhaps more suitable for inclusion elsewhere in this book. Nonetheless, I can't pass up the opportunity to chide the report-crazy and statistic-hungry bureaucrats up the line. (It goes without saying that if you are a battalion commander, the bureaucrats are at the brigade or division headquarters; if you are a division commander, the bureaucrats are at corps or FORSCOM; and if you are at FORSCOM, the bureaucrats are in the Pentagon; and it doesn't end there, as anyone who has ever served in the Pentagon is well aware. What we do know with a great degree of certainty is that the bureaucrats are never us; "they" are always others at the next or higher level.)

At any rate, a very wise man, one Sir Josiah Stamp, who was a member of England's version of the Internal Revenue Service in the theoretically simpler days of 1869 to 1919, said this about administration:

> The government are very keen on amassing statistics. They collect them, add them, raise them to the nth power, take the cube root and prepare wonderful diagrams. But you must never forget that every one of these figures comes in the first instance from the village watchman, who puts down what he damn pleases.

Substitute the proverbial "company clerk with a stubby pencil" (who is always in someone else's outfit—not mine) for "the village watchman" and you have brought that quote up to date.

One final note from General Abrams: "Department of the Army should not try to fill squad leaders' slots; DA should try to do at DA only what needs to be done at DA level."

And that summarizes management better than I can.

Like hens' teeth, meetings should be few and far between.

Meetings

A meeting can be a ridiculous waste of time and money. To find part of the cost, multiply the number of participants by the length of the meeting by each person's hourly wage, and you have a part of the cost of a meeting; add utilities, transportation, per diem, and you get a better idea. But a meeting can be a smoothly run, fast-paced, agenda-controlled conference at which information is distributed (orally or written), ideas are exchanged, and conclusions are drawn.

One type of meeting is almost a must. A commander has a great need for routine, regular "commanders conferences" to pass out orders to his staff and his commanders, to put out information, to gather information, and occasionally to try out new ideas. He may very properly ask for comments on various courses of action in order for him to make up his mind. But he doesn't take a vote. He considers the alternatives and then makes a decision. These conferences are necessary, but the senior commander must run them himself with speed, an agenda, and a time limit.

There are other kinds of meetings, though, that are convened by an action office. These, too, may be necessary, but they must be carefully controlled. The action officer may have a problem to solve and need staff representations from other staff sections or even other services.

In running meetings, I have found the following principles to be worthwhile, adaptable to a PTA gathering, a seminar, a staff conference, or a commanders session.

For a commanders conference, the CO should

1. Write his own agenda, with staff input, and distribute copies, if necessary, to subordinates and staff.

2. Stick to the agenda.

3. Have a recorder write up the minutes.

4. Limit comments by a clear requirement to stick to the subject.

5. Forbid smoking.

6. Start and end the meetings at the announced time. The CO *must* be on time. That requirement derives from courtesy, but it also saves valuable time.

For staff or other officer meetings, the officer in charge of the session should

1. Prepare and distribute the subject of the meeting and the agenda.

2. Stick to the agenda.

3. Periodically sum up the points under discussion and the agreement reached.

4. Spell out disagreements clearly.

5. Set up meetings only for important discussions of problems that can be consummated no other way.

6. Strictly limit the number of attendees.

7. Start and end the meeting on time.

8. Most significantly, consider before ever calling a meeting: Is this meeting necessary?

Make them clear and brief.

Messages

We could eliminate a lot of wasted time if the telephone had never been invented. We could save a lot of money if perhaps our communications equipment were not so sophisticated and extensive. We could improve the clarity of our message traffic if we had to write out all transmissions on a message pad and transmit them via Morse code. All of this would also force decentralization of our operations to the man who has the facts and the resources. (The obverse of the above statements are also true—that the telephone properly used saves time and that today's communication gear is a lot faster than punching out a message with a key and Morse code.)

Nonetheless, there is one principle I think deserves almost rigid adherence: Always try to deliver a message to the person for whom it is intended—not a subordinate. Relaying an oral message through even one other person is an almost certain way to garble the message. I have always asked my staff for answers in writing (handwritten is good enough) rather than an oral reply—generally speaking, that is. Oral messages have a way of getting lost, of being inexact, variously interpreted, off-the-cuff, or of not being recoverable in their original form at a later date. When one writes, one is more exact and more succinct than when one speaks.

There is, of course, another side to this coin. I was the XO of a division artillery in Germany commanded by a very action-oriented BG who insisted that the staff always answer his questions orally. He disliked paperwork intensely. Somehow, he succeeded in accomplishing his goals—at least during that phase of his career—with oral answers. After he rose to the position of Vice Chief of Staff of the Army, the answers to his questions were no longer totally oral. My guess is that the questions may have become somewhat more complicated and controversial and the answers less than brief.

135

In spite of my own dislike for bureaucrats and paperwork, my experience with messages is this: Make messages short, factual, written, and delivered to the person for whom they are intended. Of course, I must admit with some reluctance that the telephone is here to stay. By all means, try to talk to the person for whom the message is intended. That way the message at least is direct and unlikely to be too badly distorted.

Communications

Unknown drill sergeant, 1917 vintage:
"The Army isn't what it used to be; in
fact, it never has been."

Military, What's Wrong with Being?

Gen. Maxwell Taylor, in the February 1973 issue of *Army,* talked articulately about the military profession as a way of life. He said it this way:

> Army life, in my opinion, should not be an extension of the civilian life which lies just over the fence of the military reservation, but something quite different which reflects the unique requirements of military life.
>
> I am unalterably opposed to the concept that the Army is merely a segment of American society which wears a uniform but which otherwise should live as nearly as possible as civilians live.
>
> But I can defend a lot of spit and shine on the basis of the effect of the personal appearance of a soldier on the taxpayers who support our armed forces . . . but one wonders whether there is any barrier which cannot be overcome by the officer who is deeply and sincerely concerned about the welfare of his men. Such concern cannot be feigned; it must be the real thing . . . an officer's insignia of grade is not a badge of privilege but one of servitude to his men.

Another facet of this theme, the "duty and the honor" that attaches to the military life, was highlighted in a speech made by Newton D. Baker, President Wilson's secretary of war:

> Men may be inexact or even untruthful in ordinary matters and suffer as a consequence only the disesteem of their associates or even the inconvenience of unfavorable litigation. But the inexact or untruthful soldier trifles with the lives of his fellow men and the honor of his government.

When one considers that the freedom, the security, the way of life of the United States depends on the quality of our military establishment, one begins to realize that the military service, especially leadership positions therein, is a high calling, a vocation not unlike the priesthood, a profession that transcends the ordinary and mundane. The military as a way of life is far different than any other profession for one profound reason: In our business we, whether we wish to admit it or not, are training men to kill other men in battle, while, at the same time, preserving the lives of our own troops.

There are many traditions, customs, and practices that, taken together, form the military way of life. Parades, ceremonies, uniforms, medals, bands, flags, close-order drill, marches are part and parcel of the way of life of a soldier and an officer. Some of them may be anachronistic: After all, we no longer, like Frederick the Great, wheel our troops into line and win battles by the precision of our maneuvers. We no longer need a reveille gun to awaken the troops in barracks or a retreat gun to call them back to the security of the fort for the night. And I suppose a case could also be made for the fact that uniforms need not be uniform (the Continental Army was a ragtag outfit, by uniform standards, when compared to the precisely uniformed and elegantly turned-out British Redcoats. And the VC and NVA were not particularly natty.)

Nonetheless, all of these practices and traditions do go to make up our military way of life. Yet we are allowing the military to degenerate into a nine-to-five, five-day-a-week, civilian-type organization with civilian attitudes about overtime, breaks, and conditions. This is drastically wrong. The military must be above that approach. We must insist upon the standards we have learned the hard way, over many generations of officers and men. Those are standards of discipline, training, dedication, and concern. We should not have to learn that over and over again after each war; we should learn from the past. Hindsight is 20/20.

In more specific terms, what I am advocating is a return of the troops to life in open-bay barracks and away from their pads in nearby communities; a return of authority to the NCOs where it belongs; a return to the traditional trappings of the military: sharp uniforms, precise formations, frequent inspections of living and work areas; a return to discipline and the punishment of recalcitrants; a return to stockades (as opposed to easy outs) if necessary; a return to a demand for the achievement of high standards in all things—the mess, the supply room, the orderly room, the barracks —a return to soldiering as a way of life.

There is such a thing; be proud of it.

Mind, Military

From time to time in history, the hue and cry goes up over the "man-on-horseback" syndrome. Even our own Constitution made certain that the Commander-in-Chief of the military establishment would be an elected official, the President of the United States. The secretary of defense and the secretaries of the services are appointed civilians. Thus, the hierarchy managing and administering the military in the United States is definitely civilian-controlled.

Many other countries have been subjected to military dictatorships of the right; many still are. Military dictatorships are traditionally repressive, freedom-strangling, and totally unacceptable to a freedom-loving people. Unfortunately, many writers, historians, and politicians equate all military men with authoritarianism, rigidity of thinking, repressiveness, despotism, and arrogance.

It is true that in the military, where men are taught to kill or be killed, where life in combat is dangerous, dirty, and miserable, vote-taking and arbitration have no part. Discipline must be hard but fair, men must do what they are told to do, and training must be continuous, professional, and demanding. But all that is not to say that a military professional is hidebound, inflexible, dictatorial, unfeeling, and tunnel-visioned.

The true military mind is one trained to solve problems with logic, objectivity, wisdom, and speed. The military mind is taught to identify a problem, break it down into its component parts, consider all the facts, look at the alternatives, weigh the pros and the cons, and then make a decision. The military mind is taught to do the harder right instead of the easier wrong, that integrity is a supreme virtue, that protecting one's men is a dominant theme in the scheme of things, and that there is nothing wrong in being a perfectionist—so long as one does not get lost in the forest of details.

140

The military mind is logical, objective, hard-nosed when necessary, blunt when demanded, considerate. It is not motivated by profit, except in the sense that a military mind must try to arrive at a solution that is most efficient of time, people, and resources. In that sense, profit does enter the equation. But it is not profit for the individual; it is profit for the entire organization.

Develop a military mind; be proud of it.

And on the lighter side, here's an old Irish saying: "You can refuse to love a man and you can refuse to lend him money, but if he wants a fight, then you have to oblige him." Now, that's a military mind.

A mission is a unit's steering wheel.

Missions

There can be no doubt that a unit with a mission, which knows what it is supposed to do, trains to do just that, and knows that what it is doing is important, is a productive, dedicated, and reasonably trouble-free unit. Simply stated, it has high morale.

Time and again, one sees this seemingly paradoxical phenomenon. For example, the USAR 866th Repair Parts Company was on active duty for its annual reserve training at Fort Carson, Colorado, recently. I dropped in, unannounced, to see them and said in an aside to my aide as we were driving to the unit: "How would you like to command this outfit? Doesn't it remind you of the hypothetical mess kit repair outfit with which no one could do anything?" The aide, fresh from commanding an airborne, gung ho infantry company, said: "No way would I like to be mixed up with this crowd."

Nonetheless, when we visited the unit, we found an outfit deep into its work, fully occupied during the entire training time, well versed in the various regulations that governed its operations, and with high morale. The troops were in sharp uniforms and the NCOs and officers very military. The unit was proud of what it was doing. Why? Because it had a mission. It was this: The senior commander for whom they worked assigned the unit the mission of being responsible for the repair parts supply for his entire 9,000-man organization year-round—not just on annual training. Thus, the unit felt needed and important; it had a clear-cut, important mission to perform; its dedication to its task was the result. It must also have been blessed with some outstanding NCOs and officers.

Another aspect of mission accomplishment involves assigning one unit a mission regardless of the type of work involved. No matter what the job—police, patrol, other off-the-wall details—

the best way to accomplish any given task is to assign it to one unit of the appropriate size working under its own NCOs and/or officers. This is far superior to asking for a detail of men from various units and putting them under a randomly selected NCO or officer.

Finally, the third feature of mission involves accepting as many of them as possible and doing them all. A well-organized unit can do a great many more things than one would have thought possible. At Fort Riley, Kansas, when I was the commander of the First Infantry Division, we were in the throes of readying the division for its annual seven-week fall trip to Europe for Exercise REFORGER. Nonetheless, during the summer preceding that deployment, the division was assigned such missions as running the Summer Camp for some four thousand ROTC cadets, testing the Maverick Missile for the Air Force, conducting a rifle marksmanship contest for the Fifth Army, and running a test of a new training concept. All these missions were in addition to the myriad tasks that the division had to do routinely. We accepted all the missions and finally requested higher headquarters to call a halt only when I felt that we had saturated the troops and facilities.

The various aspects of peacetime mission assignment and accomplishment came together brilliantly for the spectacular military display and demonstration that welcomed President Kennedy to Fliegerhorst Kaserne, Hanau, Germany, in June of 1963. CG, USAREUR, assigned the overall mission to the CG of 5th Corps, a meticulous, military, imaginative man not given to doing things halfheartedly or in a slovenly manner. On the contrary, he knew the full meaning of spit and polish.

The commander of the corps assigned to the 3d Armored Division one part of the overall display: setting up the Honor Guard. But this was no ordinary Honor Guard. It consisted of twenty-five battalions from throughout the theater, aligned precisely along the Fliegerhorst Airfield, a thousand-man color guard (250 sets of colors) in the center of the formation, five bands along the lines of troops, and six rows of tanks, self-propelled artillery, APCs, engineer equipment, and Honest Johns and other missiles behind the line of troops.

In addition, on another ramp of the airfield, there was a separate detachment for arrival honors. It consisted of a platoon of

Americans, one of Germans, one of Canadians, a firing battery for the salute, and another band.

At the time, I was the CO of the 3d Armored Division Artillery in Hanau. The division CG assigned me two missions: (1) Take overall charge of setting up the Honor Guard and command it (the twenty-five battalions) and (2) set up a tent camp for some ten thousand troops who would be coming into Hanau from outlying kasernes and would need to be housed and fed for upwards of a week before the actual ceremony.

To set up the tent city, the division CG had allocated to me three company-sized units. I assigned each unit a specific area in which to work and then put them to work on a competitive basis to see which unit could put up the most tents properly in the shortest time. The scheme worked; the troops fell to the task with a lot of enthusiasm, the tents were up in a very short time, and the mission was accomplished in great good order. Unconsciously or otherwise, I followed the rules of mission accomplishment: Assign missions by unit, give the CO a job to do and let him do it, make it competitive.

My other mission, command of the Honor Guard, was a little more difficult to accomplish. In addition to the eighteen battalions of the 3d Armored, there was a squadron from the Air Force, a parachute battalion from the 8th Division, a battalion of Special Forces, and four corps artillery battalions.

Normally, when a division is lined up on a parade ground, it has a straight front line but a very ragged rear line because of the different numbers of men in the various battalions. Because President Kennedy was going to fly over this formation in a helicopter on his arrival, and because there would be no pass in review (the President would drive down the front line to inspect the troops and to the rear to inspect all the equipment lined up there), I persuaded the corps commander to make a rectangle of the formation by varying the width of the front of the battalion and having a uniform depth. He bought the idea. The resulting formation of troops was, I must admit immodestly, unique and quite spectacular.

Because of President Kennedy's "Ich bin ein Berliner" speech a few days before this ceremony, his popularity with the Germans and the U.S. troops was at an all-time high. Therefore, my mission was easy to accomplish—I had the full cooperation of all commanders, and the troops were eager to appear at their best. For the formation, they were proud and standing tall even though some of them had been on line two hours before the President's arrival. But they were "spit and polish" all the way.

After his return to Washington, President Kennedy wrote of the Honor Guard ceremony: "It was one of the finest military formations I have ever seen." The troops loved that accolade.

So there it is; all the elements of getting a job done well were there:

1. Mission was clearly stated.

2. Units were available to do the job.

3. Units were assigned missions—not details selected randomly from various units.

4. Units competed against one another.

5. Troops were enthusiastic, keyed up, and proud.

Result? Mission accomplished.

Forward observer, 1984

Admit them.

Mistakes

In dealing with mistakes, one should remember another of the adages of that master of succinct truths, General Abrams. "Bad news does not improve with age."

When one makes a mistake (like not reporting bad news), one should try to rectify the situation by getting it out in the open rather than trying to conceal it.

The boss's initial reaction to an admitted mistake or error may be apoplectic, but if he is worth his salt, he'll realize upon calming down that it is far better for him to know the truth as soon as possible rather than to make a poor decision, possibly involving men's lives, based on erroneous information, faulty communications, or out-and-out mistakes. To conceal an error is grossly unfair to the entire organization. Military operations are replete with examples of lives and battles lost because of mistakes and faulty, incomplete, or off-the-cuff information.

When I was commanding a parachute artillery battalion during the Korean War, one of my batteries fired a short round wounding some of our own troops. As soon as I discovered it, I so reported with some trepidation to the RCT commander, Brig. Gen. W. C. Westmoreland.* Fortunately, he recognized the problem and took a less than disastrous view of the situation, largely because he heard it from me as soon as it happened rather than through channels from the infantry unit involved. That commander had every right to be outraged and properly let me know of his displeasure in no uncertain terms when I went to apologize to him and the unit involved. Naturally, I took some immediate and drastic steps to prevent repetition of such an error—an artilleryman's nightmare.

*Most regiments are. of course, commanded by colonels. During the Korean War, however, the separate 187th RCT was habitually commanded by a brigadier general.

The forging of the chain of command.

Morning Parade

In the Army and in this book, you have heard and read a great deal of discussion about the need to use the chain of command, about the value of the NCOs and the necessity to get them involved in the operation of their units, about the need to decentralize, about the need for NCOs to know and to look after their men, and about the necessity for the troops to know who their bosses are. How? Many of these principles can be practiced and exercised with morning parade.

Admittedly, the Morning Parade is an adaptation of a British Army tradition. It has been used in various forms and under diverse names in the American Army for decades. But it has been only recently that some commanders have used it with great success and called it Morning Parade.

I like to think that its genesis in the modern Army began back in 1971 in the Big Red One when I was its commander. In those days, we, the troop leaders in the field, were force-fed, like it or not, various gimmicks, tests, experiments, and searches for ways to make the modern volunteer Army an "exciting, interesting, and fun-filled place for soldiers to spend and enjoy their enlistments." We were seemingly more concerned with exploring such things as "adventure training," "Sunshine Houses," the "Open-Door Policy," "rap sessions," multicolored barracks, and "enlisted committees and advisors" than we were with hard training, combat-readiness, and soldiering.

One day, the head of the MVA Project at DA visited Fort Riley and had breakfast with my brigade commanders and me. Among other things, he suggested that the BRO try Morning Parade, which the British habitually and universally use in their Army. (He had recently visited England and come back with this idea, among others.) I felt, before I heard the full explanation of "Morning Parade," that it was just another worthless artifice dreamed up by "The Army Is Fun" boys in the Pentagon. I must have expressed my doubts and lack of interest, because the SOFTP (senior officer from the Pentagon) suggested that I shut up and listen to what he had to say and because the brigade commanders became suddenly silent. Since the SOFTP was a lieutenant general, one rank my senior, I decided that, even in the days of MVA, I should shut up and listen.

What he proposed I try in one of my battalions was so much along the lines of what I was trying to instill in the 1st Division that I said: "No, sir, I won't try it in one battalion; from today on, it becomes SOP in the entire division." The SOFTP nodded pleasantly, and so it came to pass that Morning Parade became part of the routine of the BRO at Riley and even in Europe on REFORGER III, and I began to change my attitude toward the MVA thinkers and movers. Maybe they weren't so dumb after all. (Remember: It's always at the next higher level where you find those nameless, meddlesome, misguided, and witless bureaucratic staffers.)

Morning Parade schedule (and there are obviously many adaptations and variations depending upon weather, field or garrison location, training program, and so on) went like this. (After breakfast. This is debatable. But if you do it before breakfast you must start an hour earlier, and it's hard to get troops fed and on to training afterwards. I much preferred to have Morning Parade after breakfast.)

0700   Troops fall out in company-sized units. No officers present. NCOs inspect their troops, check attendance, report to the first sergeant.

0710   Company commander arrives, takes report from the first sergeant, discusses day's activities with the company, makes announcements.

0720   Company commander departs. First sergeant and NCOs conduct school of the soldier, close-order drill in squad, platoon, or company-sized formation depending upon the level of training.

0740   NCOs conduct physical training for the company.

0750   All officers join the company for a two- to four-mile run (length again depending upon the level of fitness of the company). Troops return to barracks and get ready for the day's activities.

0830   Normal training commences. Meanwhile, while NCOs are conducting close-order drill and PT, the officers are meeting with their commander to finalize assignments, training, administration and inspect the barracks, supply, mess.

Often, when a commander starts Morning Parade in his unit, he finds that the NCOs have forgotten how to give commands and that they are timid with their soldiers. After a few months, however, the weak NCOs are weeded out, the troops have an idea of who their bosses are, the NCOs have a much closer relationship with their soldiers, and the entire chain of command begins to function. In addition, of course, the troops are in much better shape, they look better, the barracks are improved, and the entire organization begins to take on a very military appearance. And perhaps not amazingly, morale, esprit, and discipline markedly improve. Battalion and company commanders can inaugurate this system on their own—even if the major unit hasn't gotten around to it.

One of the brigade commanders in the BRO in those days eventually commanded a division, a corps, and eventually FORSCOM. He wrote to me one time to say, tongue-in-cheek, that in his corps he had developed and implemented a marvelous method for getting the troops started properly each day. He said that he had also thought up a good term for it: He called it Morning Parade. Naturally, I congratulated him on his intelligence, initiative, and soldierly proclivities. Morning Parade is a return to basic blocking and tackling.

NCOs

The NCO is a many-faceted human being: He may be a grizzled, tough, profane, hairy-chested, ham-handed archetype of a first sergeant; he may be a fuzzy-cheeked, highly educated technician; he may be a "dese and dose" grade-school dropout; he may be an eminently well qualified manager in a crucial sergeant major slot; he may be weak or strong, loved or despised, hard-drinking or teetotaling, articulate or bumbling. But whatever his pedigree, educational experience, lifestyle, or persuasion, the Army would be an unworkable, undisciplined, out-of-control mass of unguided bodies without its NCOs.

The model of the career NCO, in my view, was the sergeant major of the 1st Infantry Division at Fort Riley in 1971: Command Sgt. Maj. Carlos Leal. He started his career, as he liked to tell it modestly, as an insignificant mortar ammunition bearer in the 82d Airborne Division during World War II. His education was limited to the eighth grade, but his innate intelligence, drive, and dedication were limitless. He served a number of tours in Vietnam with Special Forces on extremely hazardous missions deep in VC territory. His courage and bravery under fire were legendary.

When I met him, he was the sergeant major of the JFK Center at Bragg that I had just been assigned to command. After that tour, I was named to be CG of the 1st Division. Sergeant Major Leal asked to come along. I hastened to accept his offer before he could change his mind when he realized he wouldn't be on jump status in the 1st Division. By a few weeks after his arrival, he was a prominent figure. The sergeants major of subordinate units would rather have a visit from me than from Carlos. He wasn't arrogant, rude, or dictatorial. He just knew what was right, he set high standards for the appearance of the troops and for the police and maintenance of the barracks and housing areas, and he demanded superb performance from his fellow NCOs. He knew them and understood them. He was on duty twenty-four hours a day, seven days a week. His advice to me was wise, understanding, and full of the soldierly wisdom of a career in the Army. He knew what the troops wanted. He organized a skydiving club, a motorcycle club, drag racing, and a host of other things to keep the troops busy with wholesome pursuits. His son graduated from West Point as the captain of the national intercollegiate champion sports parachuting team and a highly respected cadet battalion commander. Carlos left the BRO in the summer of 1972 to return to his first love—the Special Forces. He died inexplicably (at least to me) making his third jump of the morning (and about the 2,500th of his career) in Thailand after he left the 1st Division. He was truly a giant among NCOs and a man I considered a close friend.

A success story, not only for the NCO Corps, but for the Army as a whole, is the case of an ex–WW II NCO who is now a four-star general and the Chairman of the Joint Chiefs of Staff. Gen. Jack Vessey is one of the foremost examples of how intelligence, drive, and military know-how pays off in the Army. He commanded one of my 3d Armored Division artillery battalions back in 1963–64. He is a superb soldier and man.

And still another: A major general who worked for me in the Pentagon was only a high school graduate when he entered the Army. He went through the ranks from private to permanent major general and, along the way, earned a Ph.D. from the Harvard Business School.

But it is the unsung, hard-working, dedicated, compassionate leader of men, the career NCO, on whom the Army depends. He knows where the bodies are buried, he knows the problems of the troops, he knows how to get things done, he knows how to advise and assist his commander.

But he doesn't spring full-grown and mature from the ranks of the PFCs; he has to be taught and trained, nurtured and aided, respected and sought after, counseled and challenged, heeded and valued, honored and appreciated.

In the 82d Airborne Division today, as it is in many of today's outfits, the NCO is responsible for the conduct of the troops, their military courtesy, their behavior, and their overall condition. The chain goes from the division sergeant major down to the squad leader.

The Army cannot function without its NCOs; that's why NCOs are the backbone of the Army and the skeleton on which all else is hung. The Army is only as good as its skeleton; therefore, the NCO is of paramount, absolute importance.

Necessity—and lack of funds—is the mother of invention.

Nothing, Something for

In these days when the Army is spending vast sums of money for equipment and for the pay of its soldiers and civilian workers (28.5 percent of the Army's recent budget is for the pay of people, 29 percent for the purchase of new equipment), there is relatively little left over for the support of recreational projects for the benefit of the troops and their dependents on a post. Nonetheless, there are many opportunities to provide benefits at little or no cost. For example:

Drag racing? Use the post airfield on weekends.

POV repair? Use the maintenance facilities on off-duty hours.

Parachuting? Set up a sports parachute club.

Motorcycling? Set up a cross-country run on a range.

Flying? Set up a flying club; there are plenty of flying instructors.

Children's activities? Many soldiers are more than willing to organize and supervise.

Running? Set up races of various lengths (10,000 meters, 25,000 meters, marathons) on post.

Athletic tournaments? Set them up in tennis, golf, softball, touch football, volleyball, squash, handball, racquetball.

Some of these may not be particularly adaptable or within the purview of a company or battalion commander. But many others are. An imaginative commander and staff officer can come up with an almost endless list.

When I was commanding a battery in New Guinea before we went into combat in the Philippines, the first sergeant set up an athletic field behind the battery line of tents for touch football, softball, volleyball, etc. We had many contests there, both intra-battery and with other teams from nearby units.

153

After we landed on Bito Beach in Leyte but were not yet committed to combat, again the first sergeant found a place for volleyball on the beach. The second day we were there a kamikaze came roaring down the beach toward our bivouac area, and we scattered for the palm trees. But he was not interested in us; over our position, he did a 90-degree turn to the right, took a few antiaircraft rounds in his fuselage, but never wavered. He flew directly and unerringly into the bridge of a transport off-loading about fifteen hundred meters off shore and sank the ship. Thereafter we used the hulk as an aiming point for possible firing against an alleged Japanese naval and marine force that, intelligence had it, was due to land on Bito Beach at any moment. The landing never came. Kamikazes have little to do with volleyball games on the beach, I know. Nonetheless, the attack was a diversion and one none of us will ever forget.

The point is that a commander does not need special services officers, athletic directors, or other highly paid technicians to keep the troops occupied. The Army today provides a variety of facilities for all sort of off-duty pursuits for education, athletics, and recreation. Find out what they are and use them to the utmost. It will pay great dividends.

Targets, goals, ends—every unit needs them.

Objectives

No matter what the operation—a squad in the attack, a division in defense, a training program, a football game, a maintenance program, preparation for inspection—one must have an objective and a time frame, both of which must be clearly defined, before one can get on with a task. Otherwise, a unit or a staff mucks about aimlessly and indifferently.

In civilian circles, there have been many seminars held and endless books published on the subject of management. Among other techniques, there are Management by Exception (worry only about those things that are apt to or are going wrong—the squeaky wheel technique) and Management by Objective, MBO (set objectives— let everyone in on the act—more like management by committee). But no matter what they call it, the civilian management experts are finally recognizing, however dimly and partially, what military planners and commanders have known and practiced for a long time, at least since the days of Miltiades at the Battle of Marathon in 490 B.C. What the management experts are finally coming to realize is that a business, a work team, an individual must have an objective and a time-phased plan to achieve it. What the civilian management experts sometimes do not fully understand is organizational techniques, particularly a chain of command.

Back in the World War II days of airborne, we used a planning system known as backward planning (which was later changed to Reverse Planning because of the obvious derogatory connotation of the former title). In this planning system, the staff started to plan an operation, first of all, focusing on the objective or objective area and the mission. Then, the staff determined the size of the airborne force needed and the time by which the force must be on the objective. Next, the staff figured out how long it would take to get from the DZs to the objective; they then calculated how long it would take to assemble the force on the DZ; then, they had to figure out when the first man had to exit the first plane; next, they had to determine the time length of the aircraft columns; then, they put in the plan the time needed to take off and assemble in the air all of the gliders and transports; next, they had to figure out how long it would take to move the troops from the bivouac areas to the departure field. Finally, the planning staff published the whole schedule in reverse of the way they had planned it so that subordinate units knew when they had to leave their bivouac areas, when they had to draw parachutes, when they had to load up the aircraft, and so on. By this time, the planners were reduced to hoping for good weather and that the pathfinders were on time on target. They had to figure that into their calculations, also. And it all started with an objective.

Basically, the same system applies to any operation. It's a matter of learning from your superior what it is that he wants you to do and by when he wants it; then it's up to you to do the planning—in your head for a simple matter or on reams of paper for a large operation.

One of the larger, easily defined, one-objective tasks in which I played a part was the establishment of the Vietnamese Defense College.

In 1967 in Vietnam, after I had served a short tour as ADC of the 25th Division, I was assigned the job of Director of the Training Directorate, MACV (for training of ARVN). One bright, sunny day in September, I rode out to Tan Son Nhut with COMUSMACV, who was about to leave on a trip to the U.S. He stopped by the quarters of the prime minister and, when he came out, told me that he wanted me to establish a National Defense College for RVN. With a great show of bravado and a confidence I didn't at that moment feel, I said: "Yes, sir. When do you want it to open?" Rather nonchalantly, as was his wont, he said, "How about February?" I gulped and said, "Yes, sir." Certainly, the objective and the date of completion were clear and concise; it was almost like the message to Garcia. All I had to do was produce.

After thinking about the objective for a few days, I decided that I needed a building, a staff, a faculty, a student body, a curriculum, a library, and money, among other things. And so I set to work. My plan used the reverse planning concept. I knew that February 1968 was the objective date, and I worked everything in reverse from there. We figured out how long it would take to accomplish each major portion of the task; then we established a starting date for each operation and set up checkpoints and a timetable so that all the disparate parts of the operation dovetailed neatly together and finished just before February. I appointed the smartest colonel I could find to carry out the plan, and then gave him his head. We had great cooperation from the MACV staff because it was a COMUSMACV project. It had great enthusiasm and support from the Vietnamese High Command because we were developing for them a prestigious institution.

At any rate, finally, all parts of the plan meshed neatly together on schedule, and by February 1968 the doors of the college in Saigon were ready to open for the first class; but just about then Tet '68 hit, and the VC were the first through the doors. Nonetheless, after we cleaned up that mess, both inside and outside the college, we enrolled the first class of senior ARVN officers in June.

I visited the college in 1970 on a trip to Saigon. It was functioning on all cylinders and had achieved a rather distinctive place in the RVN military structure. Unfortunately, we must not have taught them properly or perhaps did not have time enough to train the proper number of ranking ARVN senior officers. Today, I suppose, the NVA may be using the same facility in Ho Chi Minh City for less admirable purposes. I do hope the Russians are conducting seminars on how to develop an economy or how to increase agricultural production, at both of which they are singularly inept.

What all this boils down to is this: Regardless of the task, no matter the level of the unit or staff, the two most important parts of any assignment are (1) the objective and (2) the completion date. With these two basics, a commander or a staffer can function.

All officers are classifiable—one way or another.

Officer Evaluation (German-style)

For some years, a supposedly true story of how the old, pre–WW II German General Staff evaluated the German Army officers has been a part of the lore of officers of my vintage. The origin of the story is lost in the vague recesses of the past and may be just as apocryphal as the Hitler diaries. But fictitious or not, the story describes an officer evaluation technique that has a good deal of validity.

When one attempts to categorize one's officers (or NCOs) and/or write efficiency reports about them, one is occasionally stumped for descriptive words, categories, or levels of competence by which to characterize them. This is especially true at the battalion and company level, where commanders have the rare opportunity of knowing their men well under all kinds of military and social situations. Therefore, the German General Staff method may help young commanders fit their officers and NCOs into convenient and easily imagined pockets.

According to the legend, the German General Staff (which was a separate entity and a total career assignment for some German Army officers), with a tradition of many wars over the years interspersed with some fleeting moments of peace, evolved a rating system based on the staff's conclusion that all officers had basically two fundamental and inherent characteristics in varying degrees: intelligence and energy. Using only these two characteristics, then, the General Staff classified all officers into four categories and assigned them according to those evaluations:

1. The smart and industrious: They became staff officers.
2. The smart and lazy: They became commanders.

158

3. The dumb and lazy: They drifted into liaison officer slots.

4. The dumb and industrious: The story goes that the General Staff had them shot because they were dangerous, unassignable, and useless, but in all probability, they became commanders of stalags.

I'm not suggesting that you assign your officers or NCOs according to the German General Staff classifications; obviously there are many gradations of intelligence and industry among people, but the GGS system has a lot of merit and can provide you a general outline for mentally, at least, pigeonholing your subordinates.

Division review

An acceptable chain-of-command violator
—occasionally.

Officers Call

One of the time and tradition-honored ways for a unit commander to get "the word" to his officers is at the unit officers call. This is done frequently at the company and battalion level, less frequently at the brigade level, and perhaps only semi- or less annually at the division level.

But at whatever level, the unit commander, not a staff officer or executive officer, must be in charge of the meeting. This is the commander's call, so to speak, and he should use the opportunity to talk to his officers about his policies, ideas, plans, and instructions. It violates the chain of command, in a sense, but if used judiciously, it is a superb way not only to communicate but to let junior officers get to know the boss—or at least his policies.

Like any other meeting, the most important thing to remember is that you have assembled a number of officers and/or men at some considerable cost in man-hours and convenience. Therefore, the subject of the meeting must be important enough to merit that kind of expense. Only you, the commander, can decide that. And just as for any other decision you make, you must consider the pros and cons and be guided thereby.

Many commanders call their officers together at, say, 1600 hours on a Friday afternoon and then, after meeting, adjourn to the Officers' Club for Beer Call. I have always found it congenial and sociable to have such sessions and to have the wives present at the Club. Then, if there are any minor or semiserious awards to be presented (birthday notices, wedding anniversaries, babies, hails and farewells, etc.) to either wives or officers, the commander has a perfect forum. (I'm not suggesting I invented Beer Call; I'm just reminding you that it's a great idea regularly to do so.)

Open-Door Policy

One of the ideas that came out of the early days of the VOLAR program, when we experimented with a number of innovative and sometimes radical notions, was the so-called open-door policy. Basically, this meant that a CO had an open door to whoever wanted to see him for any reason without having to go through the chain of command.

This system is clearly a flagrant violation of the chain of command. Why, for example, should a soldier talk to his platoon sergeant when he can amble up to division headquarters and see the division commander? Or to battalion and walk in and see the battalion commander?

The Army has all kinds of ways for a soldier to air his grievances or other problems (the IG, chaplain, Red Cross, ACS are some). But the man who should be looking after the welfare of the troops, handling their problems, and assisting in getting them solved is the troopers' immediate leader. And that leader is the one who either solves the legitimate problem or takes it to the staff officer or commander who can solve it.

The open-door policy is great at the squad and perhaps platoon level; after that, the chain of command takes over.

I can't think of anything more detrimental to good order and military discipline than the open-door policy. I trust by now that it has gone the way of wrap leggings and iron wheels for the Pack–75s.

*A commander's responsibility and
a soldier's right.*

Pay

In the old days—before automation, computers, and JUMPS—
payday was a once-monthly event of some significance to both the
commander and the troops. In many units, the commander inspected his troops in ranks before the actual "payday activities."
(On paydays the troops were present; they needed the money.)
After the inspection, the troops lined up, snaked their way into the
orderly room or mess hall, saluted the pay officer smartly, reported
properly, signed the payroll, and then moved on down the line of
other desks where various collectors (laundry, mess, contributions,
etc.) took large and small bites out of the relatively small pay that
the soldier then received. After that, the soldier had the rest of the
day off, ostensibly to pay his bills downtown, go to the commissary, and/or hand over to his wife whatever remained of his pay.
However, crap tables and poker games in various barracks rooms
were strong enticements for the soldier to delay his departure for
those far more important but far less attractive errands. And, thus,
many soldiers were broke shortly after they left the pay table, crap
game, or the EM or NCO club. But in those days, the majority of
soldiers ate in the mess hall, lived in barracks, wore GI uniforms,
and were reasonably content but broke until the end of the next
month.

All that is a thing of the past, of course. One of the more beneficial results of computers is the Army's automated pay system. It's
fast and, today, reasonably accurate. In the early days of JUMPS,
there were far too many errors and snafus in the system. But by the
inauguration of a series of checks (the triple check system was
devised and implemented in the 82d Airborne Division Pay Section),
payroll error rates were reduced to miniscule portions.

Today, no pay officer is needed, for the most part. The soldier's

162

check goes either directly to him or to an account at his bank. The pay table is a thing of the past—along with canvas leggings, Sam Browne belts and, unfortunately, pinks and greens.

But that does not relieve the commander of the responsibility of ensuring that his troops are paid properly and on time. Computers may be infallible, but there are still humans in the system who must make the initial inputs. Fortunately, these days, their pencils are a little less stubby.

Five miles a day keeps the doctor away.

Physical Fitness

The Army traditionally has emphasized the physical fitness of its troops. In some units, the attitude toward physical fitness of members is almost religious: The Rangers, Airborne, and Special Forces have doted on long runs, marathon marches, highest standards for fitness tests, and long and arduous field exercises in the cold of Alaska, the heat of California's desert, and the Calcasieu swamp of Fort Polk.

General Westmoreland went even further. When he commanded the 187th Airborne Regimental Combat Team in Korea and Japan, the theme for the troops' fitness was "lean and mean." Before the RCT went to Korea for its third combat tour, it muscled through a "Tigerization Program," made up of equal parts of PT, indoctrination about the nastiness of the North Koreans and the Chinese, weapons qualifications, and hand-to-hand fighting skills. By the time of the armistice along the DMZ, the regiment was so combat-honed that it needed a "de-tigerization" period before it sailed back to the peacetime garrison life of Kyushu.

Today, the Airborne, Rangers, and Special Forces uphold the tradition of physically fit troops. But there are many other units not far behind. The Fit to Fight Program of the 2d Division in Korea seeks to make every man a tiger and to point out that "fatigue makes cowards." The 1st Division, the 3d Corps, and the 7th Division have at one time or another used the morning parade and its inherent PT and runs to shape up the troops.

But physical fitness shouldn't stop there. Around the world, wherever it is located, the Army should be stressing physical fitness. Every commander should have a program for himself and his troops, whether they are airborne, infantry, or "chairborne" administrative types. Running is one of the best exercises: It's good for the heart, the lungs, and stamina. And it can be a lifelong benefit. (Jack Kelley of Boston has run in fifty-one Boston Marathons and, at age seventy-six, is training for his fifty-second.)

No matter what the program (the Canadian 5BX for men and 10BX for women are splendid ones), physical fitness for his troops and himself should be of primary concern to a commander.

Physical fitness is a lifelong pursuit. Check the number of men and women over sixty who are running ten-kilometer races, semi-marathons, and even full-scale marathons. These are not extraordinary people but simply normal, everyday folks who have decided that they will not let creeping old age deprive them of their enjoyment of life. Running daily may or may not prolong your life, but it will certainly improve its quality. (I assure you that my five miles per day and hard singles tennis four or five times a week have made my retirement a lot easier to bear. And I still run ten-kilometer races with my son, who has the temerity to beat me by about ten minutes.)

The Principles of War

Throughout the ages, man has evidenced a fertile mind and a diabolical genius for inventing, developing, and mass-producing increasingly effective and potent weapons of war. Fists gave way to clubs; clubs to rocks; rocks to arrows, lances, and sabers. Almost simultaneously, catapults and battering rams arrived on the battlefields. With the introduction of gunpowder, a whole new galaxy of weapons changed the tempo and dimensions of warfare; pistols, revolvers, rifles, mortars, artillery, missiles, air-delivered bombs influenced the battle and its outcome. In terms of mobility, the soldier moved from foot, to horses, to elephants, to camels, to wagons, to motor vehicles, to aircraft. The defense vied with the offense for dominance on the battlefield: Armored knights and horses for a time held sway against the foot soldier armed with swords and bows and arrows and protected, clumsily, by hand-held shields; more recently, machine guns aided the defense until mortars and artillery blasted them out of their dug-in miniforts; antitank weapons and missiles knocked out tanks until the tanks put on more and thicker armor plate and increased their speed and mobility on the battlefield; then came better antitank weapons, and so forth and so on.

There is simply no end to man's ability to create more and more devastating weapons to defeat his real or imagined enemy's newest advances—whether on the ground, in the air, or under or on the surface of the world's oceans. For example, the newest Russian supersubmarine, the *Typhoon*, is as big as the Royal Navy's largest ship, the aircraft carrier HMS *Hermes*; the *Typhoon* carries twenty SS–N–X missiles, each containing twelve individually targeted nuclear warheads with a range of six thousand miles. Its arrival on the scene is certain to cause NATO planners migraine headaches until they figure out a way to counteract it.

Today, research and development speed on toward more and more exotic weapons and systems of defense and offense. Our weapons experts and think tanks, the prognosticators of the future, are writing, developing, and talking about a steady stream of ideas and hardware that boggle the mind and tend to make *Buck Rogers* and *Star Wars* believable.

To these futurists, the future of warfare will be underwritten by science at its deadliest best. Weapons will be electromagnetic guns that fire almost silently and hurl projectiles through the air with the speed of light; smart bombs that can home in on moving targets; man-controlled bolts of lightning to vaporize targets; gravity-collapsing beams that, at the ultimate, will turn cities into black holes; laser beams that, with deadly accuracy on and above the earth's surface, will pulverize targets in a flash of energy; and directed-energy weapons, the death rays of science fiction.

Military vehicles, tanks and troop carriers, will be more thickly armored but with lighter materials, thereby enabling them to travel on cushions of air. Natural barriers like rivers and mountains will thus become insignificant to advancing columns of armor. Aircraft will have forward-swept wings to enable them to be far more agile in the skies. Ships will skim the surface of the seas at speeds up to a hundred knots.

In intelligence and counterintelligence, science fiction comes to life. Computer surveillance will expose vast areas of the land to the eyes of military commanders and make the oceans transparent, no longer able to hide submarines in their depths. Electronic warfare will permit the opposing forces to create phantom fleets, divisions of soldiers where there are none, and aircraft immune to radar detection. Satellites in space will map forces on the ground and relay information on the enemy troops and their movements. There's talk of lasers capable of transmitting enormous amounts of data at high speed—the entire *Encyclopaedia Britannica* in one second. (I do hope that the futurists are also working to solve the problem of what to do with all that data.)

In addition to coping with electronic warfare, high-speed vehicles of all types on and above the battlefields and the oceans, and the widespread use of computers, the scientists have to think about man himself. They plan to immunize him against stress—even as they now immunize him against polio and smallpox—with a shot that will permit him to fight and function without sleep for weeks. Science might even be able to engineer him genetically (perhaps use only robots) to cope with warfare twenty-first century–style.

In just a few short years, the year 2000 and a new century will be upon us. The senior leaders of the Army of the twenty-first century have already been commissioned. Is warfare going to change so drastically that the tried and proven principles of the past will no longer apply? I think not, in spite of the apparently unrestrained but nonetheless clearly thought out visions of the futurists. Throughout the recorded history of war, from Marathon in 490 B.C. to Châlons in A.D. 451, to Hastings in 1066, to Blenheim in 1704, to Waterloo in 1815, to World Wars I and II, to the revolutions and limited wars of the post–World War II era, the principles of war have remained virtually unchanged and equally applicable.

So, for what it's worth, here they are again, arranged according to an acronym (MOSSCOMES) to help you remember them.

Mass. A commander concentrates his forces at a given point so that at that particular point, the point of decision, he has a greater combat superiority than does his enemy. He does not necessarily have a greater number of troops overall, but at the point of decision he has a greater preponderance of force. At the battle of Leuctra in 371 B.C., when the Thebans fought the Spartans, the Thebans overwhelmed a larger number of Spartans by massing at the point of decision.

Objective. A great force must have a specific and very definite objective that it must accomplish. It also may have intermediate objectives that, if accomplished, will lead to the accomplishment of the final objective. All units in a force have objectives that, taken together, keep the battle organized and on the track and eventually lead to the force's victory.

Security. Commanders must take the measures necessary to prevent surprise, to preserve freedom of action, and to deny to the enemy information of his own forces. Certainly the Japanese at Pearl Harbor meticulously followed this principle.

Surprise. The principle of surprise, of course, holds that if we do keep our plans from the enemy, if he has no idea of what our intentions are, we can achieve a greater victory than without it. We may achieve a victory out of all proportion to the power employed.

Command (Unity of Command). All the forces, regardless of service, that are put together to accomplish one common goal must be under the command of one single commander with the requisite authority. Pearl Harbor is an example of the failure to apply this failure.

Offensive. Only offensive action achieves decisive results. It permits the commander to exploit the initiative and impose his will on the enemy.

Maneuver. A commander must position his forces to place the enemy at a relative disadvantage. A commander takes advantage of weaknesses in the enemy to outmaneuver him. He takes advantage of the ability of his own forces to maneuver, to cut down his own casualties, and to inflict greater casualties and greater losses on the enemy. Maneuver alters relative combat power.

Economy of Force. This principle is the corollary to the principle of mass. It means that at points other than the point of decision a commander has only the minimum essential means. To devote means to unnecessary secondary efforts or to employ excessive means on required secondary efforts is to violate the principles of both mass and objective. The mass must be in the critical area.

Simplicity. Commanders must keep their plans as simple as possible because battle is extremely complex anyway, and the simpler the plans, the easier it is to carry them out.

There they are—the principles that have guided the great captains to victory on history's battlefields. The principles are solid and immutable and as applicable to the company and the battalion as they are to the Napoleons, MacArthurs, Eisenhowers, Pattons, and Montgomerys of other wars in other climes. Think of them in light of your past experience; visualize their applicability to the limited wars of Central America or the possible so-called modern war against a sophisticated, highly technological enemy of the future; consider them in conjunction with the Army's concept for fighting in 2000. They've worked before and they will continue to work in the future.

Make every problem a challenge.

Problem Solving

Generally speaking, no matter what the problem, there is a solution —some tough, some complicated, some easy, and some routine.

When I retired, I took a job as business manager of a nineteen-lawyer law firm in a small town in the South. The firm was very successful in spite of the fact that it had never before had a business manager; its administrative procedures were decentralized; its decisions were theoretically entrusted to various committees (personnel, library, salary, gifts, building maintenance, purchasing, etc.); its policies were unwritten and generally ad hoc, as the occasion demanded; and its financial accounting procedures were rather casual, informal, and mostly within the province of each attorney. So I had many problems to solve.

In the best military tradition, I looked to my past training to help sort out and solve the various predicaments I faced. For problem solving, I relied on two time-tested Army procedures: the staff study and the estimate of the situation. For my purposes, I combined them into one format. Whether I was developing a policy on vacations, on whether to invest in word-processing equipment, on which health insurance program to buy, on how to determine annual fee income goals for the various attorneys—no matter the problem—I relied on my old Army staff training.

Sometimes I wrote out a formal staff study; other times I simply ran it through in my own mind. But, in general, the system serves me well.

Here's the way I try to solve problems:

1. Define the problem clearly.

2. Gather the pertinent facts (for example, it may be necessary to call IBM, Lanier, CPT, or Norelco salesmen to get prices, characteristics, delivery date, performance data if the problem at hand

is the purchase of a word processor, a new copier, or even a whole new telephone system).

3. List the assumptions (here you have to be careful not to assume the problem away).

4. List possible courses of action from one extreme to the other.

5. Consider the pros and cons of each course of action (dollar cost is the most vital ingredient in a civilian enterprise).

6. Select the best course of action and either recommend implementation or do it.

Our staff colleges spend a lot of time teaching the rudiments of the staff study and the estimate of the situation. But whether or not you have been to a staff college, it's smart to use the staff study-estimate of the situation format for your problem solving.

One of the more unusual staff studies I was ever asked to write came from the G–3 of the 82d Airborne Division way back in 1948; I was the assistant G–3. The G–3 laid this one on me: "Here's the problem and here's the solution. Now write a staff study to go from one to the other." Fortunately, the whole thing tracked, and I didn't have to violate my conscience to come up with his solution. To this day, I wonder what he used that staff study for. It was not that important a problem.

Back in the dim past when I was a plebe at West Point, the wrestling coach was one "Pop" Jenkins, a legendary character around the Plain. Pop had one eye (the result, so the yarn goes, of his having been slammed into a steel corner post in a wrestling ring when he fought for the heavyweight championship of the world). At any rate, Pop summed up problem solving in words none of us ever forgot: "There ain't no holt what can't be broke." And that goes for problems.

Professionalism

In these days of highly paid athletes, actors, business managers, and TV personalities, the highest accolade that can be paid to a person in his field is to describe him as a "pro." In today's parlance, that "tells it all."

The same thing is true, of course, of the NCO or officer: One who does his job superbly is entitled to be called a pro.

But what about the so-called professional PFC or lieutenant or captain? Why must there be an "up or out" policy? What's the matter with retaining for twenty or thirty years the man or woman who is happy in the lower ranks, who can do the job in which he is placed outstandingly well, and who never causes his boss the slightest difficulty? (The British have forty-five-year-old captains who are professional company commanders.)

Retaining such "pros" in their positions would halt the progress of the "Peter Principle," which, briefly stated, holds that all persons are eventually promoted up the ladder to their level of incompetence. If we stop the Peter Principle one step before that, we keep the professional PFC, sergeant, or captain in the rank and position for which he is eminently and specifically well qualified. Thus, the Army would not have to train another man for the position, the recruiting problem would decrease, the AWOL rate would go down, and everyone, seemingly, would be happy—particularly the man or woman who is doing a splendid job in a position he or she loves.

Obviously, there is a limit to our ability to eliminate the Peter Principle. Nonetheless, there are many soldiers and officers who are well qualified to stay on their jobs even though they may never be command sergeants major or Chief of Staff of the Army.

A hundred or more to one are lousy odds.

Rap Sessions

During the early and experimental days of VOLAR, there came upon the Army scene a number of discipline-defeating aberrations, one of the worst of which was the insidious and chain of command–busting anomaly known as the "rap session." This device, theoretically to help solve the troops' problems, required a commander to assemble his troops in the day room, theater, or some other place large enough to hold them, and "rap" with the men. So far, not really a bad idea.

But, then, the rabble-rousers in the unit saw their opportunity to lead the discussion, to force their ideas on the group, to embarrass the commander, to voice absurd demands, and to take over the session. The vociferous minority thereafter ruled the session. The commander, no matter how fast on his feet, was often simply overwhelmed by the noisy minority. In essense, however, he was asking for it. There's no way he can win in such a situation. All he's doing is providing a forum for the malcontents and the gripers to voice their radical ideas and provide fun and amusement for their buddies at the expense of a chagrined and uncomfortable commander.

There are undoubtedly troops who have legitimate gripes, problems, and faults to find. But they should discuss them first with their squad (or comparable) leader and then eventually the company (or comparable) commander. It's up to the squad leader or the company commander to see to it that the legitimate complaints are heard and solved.

If that fails, the person with the problem has recourse to the IG or to the commander at the top via a letter. (See Letters to the CO.)

In sum, it is a lot better for discipline, morale, and his own well-being (but more time-consuming) for the commander to follow normal command and staff procedures than it is for him to take on his whole unit at once at a "rap session."

Regulations—Ancient, Honorable, but Still Modern

Regulations for the Discipline and Order of the Troops of the United States

29 March, 1779

Ordered that the following regulations be observed by all the troops of the United States, and that all general and other officers cause the same to be executed with all possible exactness.

By order,

John Jay, President

Attest.

Charles Thompson, Secretary

Extracts:

Chapter XV—Of the Baggage on a March.

The inconveniences arising to an army from having too great a number of wagons, must be evident to every officer; and it is expected, that for the future each officer will curtail his baggage as much as possible. . . .

Chapter XX—Of the Inspection of Men, their Dress, Necessaries, Arms, Accoutrements, and Ammunition.

The oftener the soldiers are under the inspection of their officers the better; for which reason every morning at troop beating [see Morning Parade] they must inspect into the dress of their men; see that their clothes are whole and put on properly; their hands and faces washed clean; their hair combed; their accoutrements properly fixed, and every article about them in the greatest order. . . .

174

Chapter XXIV—Of the Treatment of the Sick.

There is nothing which gains an officer the love of his soldiers more than care of them under the distress of sickness; it is then he has the power of exerting his humanity in providing them every comfortable necessity, and making their situation as agreeable as possible. . . .

Instructions for the Lieutenant.

The lieutenant,* in the absence of the captain, commands the company, and should therefore make himself acquainted with the duties of that station; he must also be perfectly acquainted with the duties of the noncommissioned officers and soldiers, and see them performed with the greatest exactness.

He should endeavor to gain the love of his men, by his attention to everything which may contribute to their health and convenience. He should often visit them at different hours; inspect into their manner of living; see that their provisions are good and well cooked, and as far as possible, oblige them to take their meals at regulated hours. He should pay attention to their complaints, and when well-founded, endeavor to get them redressed; but discourage them from complaining on every frivolous occasion.

He must not suffer the soldiers to be ill-treated by the noncommissioned officers through malevolence, or from any pique or resentment: but must at the same time be careful that a proper degree of subordination is kept up between them.

The verities of 1779, time honored and battle proven even then, are just as applicable, if not more so, today.

*It probably comes as no surprise that the word *lieutenant* is French and derives from the French words: *lieu* meaning "in place of" and *tenant*, the past participle of *tenir*, meaning "holding." Thus, a lieutenant colonel or lieutenant general is "holding in place of" a colonel or a general. Obviously, today's meaning is somewhat different because lieutenant, lieutenant colonel, and lieutenant general are ranks unto themselves.

It is not spelled "Rolaids."

Relief

Many commanders have made their macho, tough-guy, hard-line reputations based upon a penchant for relieving their subordinates peremptorily for relatively minor transgressions, errors, or omissions. Other commanders have failed to relieve their subordinate commanders even in the face of overwhelming evidence of their subordinate's incompetence, indifference, or gross malfeasance. Those of us who have been around the Army for very long can cite examples of commanders in both categories.

A commander needs to realize that his subordinates must go through a learning process, they must mature, they must somehow achieve experience even while making mistakes.

Obviously, when a subordinate commander has been given a chance to improve himself and consistently fails to do so (some officers are obviously better suited for staff than command), he should be relieved. In combat, if a commander is indecisive, unreasonable, irrational with respect to the lives of his troops, he should be relieved forthwith.

Generally speaking, however, a senior commander should consider that relief from command is a shattering, career-busting trauma for a subordinate, and he should resort to it only in the most dire circumstances. And this rule applies from platoon to Army level.

I took over my first command, B Battery of the 457th Parachute Field Artillery Battery in New Guinea in the summer (in New Guinea it didn't matter whether it was summer or winter—the heat was equally oppressive in either season) of 1944. The previous battery commander had been relieved for incompetence. His battery lacked discipline, had a high courts-martial rate, and was not particularly adept at field artillery techniques.

After a few days in command, part of the battery's problem became obvious to me—it was the first sergeant. He had no control of the battery, no idea of where the problems of the battery lay, and had immersed himself in paperwork—in those days a relatively minor administrative chore. The remedy was clear—relieve the first sergeant. In 1944, a company or battery commander had a great deal of authority; for example, I could have busted the first sergeant to private. I decided not to on the advice of the battalion commander and permitted the first sergeant to transfer in grade. It was also clear that a good part of the first sergeant's ineptness was a direct reflection of the inadequacy and inefficiency of the former BC.

In the first sergeant's stead I appointed one of the firing section chiefs—one Arthur P. Lombardi, who in later years became an RA full colonel and in airborne circles was well known as the "Godfather." It was one of the best decisions I ever made. He helped me straighten out the battery (in later years I liked to tell the Godfather's friends that I made him the first sergeant at nineteen because he could lick anybody in the battery), and later, in combat, he was among the bravest and the best. In Leyte, he and I spent a lot of time with the infantry as forward observers. He did a lot of patrolling with them and fully justified the faith I had had in him back in New Guinea. Finally, I recommended him for a battlefield commission and, by Luzon in 1945, he was a second lieutenant.

During the Korean War, when I was a battalion commander, I was forced to relieve a battery XO because his firing battery fired a short round that wounded one of our own men. I felt that under the circumstances the relief was justified. In retrospect, it may not have been, for he was not entirely responsible. I, too, may have been trying to demonstrate to the battalion what a "tough," uncompromising commander I was. I kept my eye on the young lieutenant and eventually brought him back to the battalion, where he proved his worth. He recently retired as a brigadier general.

Naturally I felt that the reliefs in the two situations I have mentioned were justified. Where I suggest you use caution is in the summary relief of a commander or NCO for a minor, one-time mistake or fault. Men can be developed; they need guidance, they need opportunities. Relief is justified only when a man repeats his errors, shows himself flagrantly lacking in judgment, or acts callous and indifferent to the lives of his men. In such cases there is only one recourse.

Research and Development

During World War II, U.S. industry produced in huge quantities a number of items that the United States supplied to itself and its allies in prodigious quantities. Just to name a few of the most battle-worthy and bug-less, the ubiquitous jeep, the workhorse 2.5-ton truck, the almost indestructible C–47, and various fighters, bomb-ers, ships of the ocean, and boats of the beach. In most cases, these items went from idea to drawing board to full-scale production in an incredibly short time. The designs were rugged, practical, and GI proof. U.S. ingenuity, imagination, and productivity, as well as our fighting men, certainly played a great role in winning World War II.

Yet in the decades since then, something seems to have hap-pened to our research and development efforts. Take the case of the jeep. We have gone through a series of models from which has evolved a jeep that is almost, but not quite, as good as the one we had in World War II. Consider the ill-fated Goat. At this writing, I think that Goats are already being phased out of the inventory. That vehicle had a short life and justifiably so. Once that mon-strosity got into the hands of the troops, it failed.

Obviously, we must go all out to develop equipment that per-forms a new function. Certainly, radar, sonar, battlefield surveil-lance equipment, the laser, night viewing devices, and various other esoteric items for use near and on the battlefield must be pursued with great interest and energy. Guided missiles, smart bombs, and various other advancements, even though extremely costly, must be developed to keep pace with our potential enemies.

One point, however, seems to have been overlooked by those involved in development over the years. Why is it necessary to make costly, time-incurring, marginal improvements in an item—such as

179

the jeep—when the new item may not be worth the effort and expense, in fact, may not even be as good as the item from which it evolved?

Simply stated, "If it ain't broke, don't fix it."

This simple maxim applies at all levels, from squad to Army, and advises against change for the sake of change. NCOs and junior officers especially must be on guard to avoid changes that just keep the troops stirred up and busy.

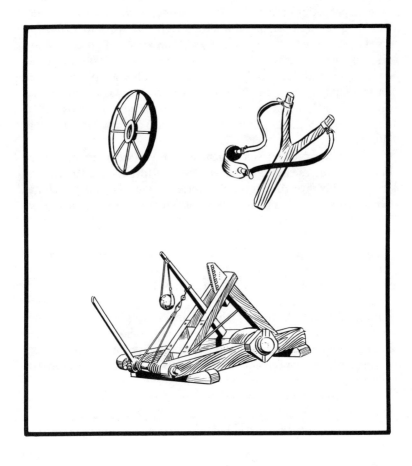

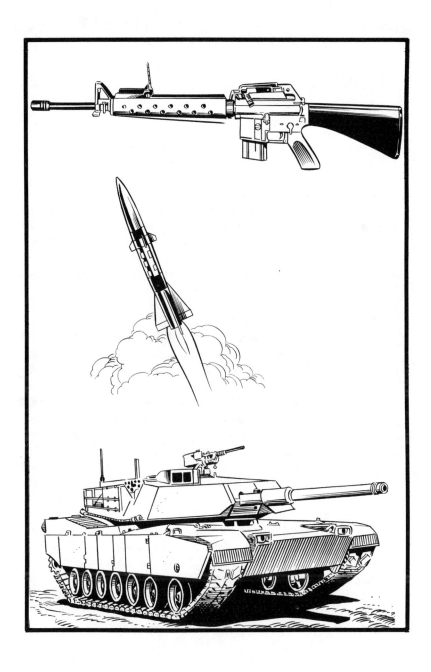

It doesn't take very long to say, "Great job."

Rewards

Material rewards for brave deeds, major accomplishments, or a lifetime of dedication to the military and to the country are difficult to find. In the military, one measures one's success by medals of various quantities, quality and rank, by promotions up the ladder from private to sergeant major or to four-star general (the latter possibility is no idle observation—at least two of today's four-star generals are OCS graduates). In civilian life, rewards are more easily measurable because of our system of free enterprise. If a businessman does a good job, he increases the profits of his company and probably qualifies for a bonus and a promotion to higher pay. His reward is obvious, real, and fairly immediate.

The military operates on a different basis from that of business and industry. What motivates a young officer, sergeant, or PFC to do a good job? Good leadership is one key motivator. Another is simply the desire to do a job well. A third is the efficiency report. A fourth is recognition in the form of letters, medals, certificates of achievement, passes, and for a unit, training holidays.

The alert commander recognizes good work from his men by one of the forms of reward available to him. If the deed is sufficiently large, it may even be a parade in honor of an individual or unit. (Secretary of Defense Laird personally came to Fort Bragg to pin medals on the men who took part in the brilliantly executed but unfortunately hollow raid on the Son Tay POW compound in North Vietnam.)

The point is this: Let a man know when he has done an excellent job. Too often a commander overlooks the man doing a good job because he is looking for the goof-off. Thus it pays a commander to look around occasionally for the hard-working good guy, give him a pat on the back, and simply say, "Great job you're doing. We really appreciate it."

Reward in public; chew in private—it bears repeating.

And also its responsibilities.

RHIP

The modern Army seems to be on a binge of egalitarianism—the difference in pay between a private and an E–5 is closing (in 1960, a sergeant major's salary was seven times as much as a recruit's; now it is about 3.5 to 1); officers and NCOs wear similar shoulder boards; privates are living in small rooms in barracks that were formerly the province of NCOs; in some areas, officers and enlisted men are sharing the same clubs; traditional customs and courtesies of the service are going by the board. Letters to the editor of *Army* even suggest that lower ranks should have the best quarters on post because the higher ranking officers to whom they are allocated are far better able to rent or buy adequate homes off post.

The awarding of privileges to NCOs and officers stems from reasonable, time-tested logic: The higher the rank, the more the responsibility and the greater should be the reward; the more the privileges, the more the desire for advancement; conversely, the fewer the advantages of increased rank, the less the desire or even need to get ahead.

In today's military establishment, because of a congressional mandate for a pay "cap," all flag officers from one- to four-star receive the same basic salary. This is the worst form of egalitarianism.

It seems to me quite obvious that as a person advances in rank, so should his privileges (within reason) and responsibilities. Why should a soldier work to get promoted if he sees that the privileges associated with the higher rank are only marginal compared with his increased responsibilities?

We need to face some basic facts: Put privates back on KP, guard, and other details; restore open-bay barracks and barracks life; stop paying men to eat off post except when necessary (travel, schools, TDY, etc.); bring back NCO privileges; make men *want* to become NCOs. Today's recruits have no idea of what they are getting for free, without having to work for it.

When the Army is strict on discipline, underprivileged youth do better. Today, because a private's pay is so high and the standards so lax, a private can move off post. He can also afford—so he thinks—to get married but ends up in squalor and on food stamps when children arrive. Living off post also ruins the camaraderie of barracks life.

So, back to basic blocking and tackling: Make NCO life more attractive than a private's life; rank does have its privileges.

These facts should not be lost on company and battalion commanders; they, too, can see to it that their NCOs have privileges commensurate with their rank.

Don't just sit there—do something.

Self-Improvement

An Army lieutenant colonel assigned to the faculty of the Naval War College a few years ago set some sort of a minor record for his activities during his first year as an advisor to the Naval Command and Staff Course, the Navy's equivalent of the Army's C&GSC at Fort Leavenworth. First, he worked for and got an M.A. in Political Science (this was a faculty-only program) from Boston University; second, he took French lessons twice a week; third, he edited a very long book on Napoleon's Guard, spending some seven hundred hours on it, for an author in Newport; fourth, he wrote a number of articles for an encyclopedia that was revising its military subjects; fifth, he won the overall squash championship of the Naval War College and the tennis championship in his age group; sixth, he wrote speeches for the president of the Naval War College (a vice admiral), particularly the president's farewell speech to the Navy, which was also the graduation address for the Naval War College; seventh, he revised a number of courses and gave instruction to students on term paper writing and speech preparation and presentation; finally, eighth, he managed to pack lunches and get breakfast for his three older children each morning while his wife was taking care of their two younger ones.

Accomplishment like this is possible by someone with ordinary intelligence and a considerable amount of drive. Admittedly, the work load in the college during the day was not very heavy. But it does prove that a man can do a lot if he tries.

Within the military there are all kinds of opportunities for self-improvement. One can take a wide variety of courses in on- and off-post schools, including graduate work. Technical courses are available in most cities for those who would train for another job.

Many roads and opportunities are available for a man and his

185

family if he will search them out and pursue his education with patience and perseverance. In other places in this book, I have cited men who have, through the Army and its educational programs, achieved great success. Commanders at lower levels should find out for themselves what courses are available on post or in nearby schools off post, and they should encourage their bright soldiers to take advantage of all the opportunities. It will pay off for the soldiers and the Army.

Reforger; culmination of training. U.S. Army photo

Keep them clear, logical, and brief.

Speeches

There are those who are born with the so-called gift of gab; there are others, brave and intrepid on battlefields and in other climes and places, who are terrified to stand up before an audience and deliver a speech; and then there are those who, after some thought and a great deal of work, are able to make outstanding speeches, even though there may be butterflies fluttering in their stomachs. Probably most people are in the latter category. Remember that the butterflies are good for you; they make you concentrate.

Many volumes have been written on how to prepare and give a speech. In spite of that, I'll go out on a limb and say that if you follow the condensed rules below you will be or can become a competent speaker.

1. Generate confidence in yourself by preparing carefully. Once you know that you know more about your subject than your audience does, most of the battle is over. Military speakers are usually assigned or asked to speak on a specific subject. That's fine because then the subject is of direct interest to the audience. If you are not asked to speak on a specific subject, select one you know will interest your audience.

2. Determine the purpose of the speech. Is it to inform, to instruct, to answer, to convert, to arouse, to influence?

3. Prepare your speech according to an outline. One helpful outline has four or six basic steps, depending upon the type of speech. The steps include *(a)* attention, *(b)* need, *(c)* satisfaction, *(d)* visualization, *(e)* action, and *(f)* summary. In a speech to inform, you need only steps *a, b, c,* and *f.*

  a. The *attention* step should do just what its name implies— it should grab the attention of your audience—but it must apply to your subject matter. An attention step may consist of relevant statistics, anecdotes, or humorous but pertinent stories. Unless your purpose is to amuse and you are an accomplished stand-up comedian, skip the jokes that have no relevance to your subject.

b. The second step is *need*. Tell your audience why they should be listening to you. Do this indirectly and discreetly; you don't have to clobber them with the fact they must pay attention.

c. Third is *satisfaction*. Satisfy the curiosity that you have aroused. This is the key and major part of a speech. Begin it with a brief, general logical outline of what it is you intend to cover, and stick to that outline. The key word here is logical. One point should follow another clearly and easily. Lead the audience through it, but give them some credit for intelligence. Sum up this part of the speech by *briefly* telling the audience what you told them.

d. Fourth is the *visualization* step. If you are trying to encourage your audience to respond in a certain way, visualize for them what that response is.

e. Fifth is the *action* step. Draw a picture in the action step of what the results will be.

f. Sixth is the *summary*. The old saw (I know I mentioned it under Briefings) about how an old southern preacher gave such good sermons applies: "I tell 'em what I'm going to tell 'em; then I tell 'em; then I tell 'em what I told 'em." Telling them what you told them is the summary.

4. Spice up a speech in a number of ways:

a. Use statistics, illustrations, and simulations, and related anecdotes.

b. Use related, pertinent jokes or stories, if time permits, but *do not overdo it*.

c. Use charts, graphs, or pictures where appropriate.

5. Remember that the best speech appeals to more than one sense. If you can show something on a screen while at the same time explaining it to your audience, you have used two senses and have simplified greatly your presentation. (Consider a speech about an apple: The best speaker in the world might be able to describe an apple, but the poorest speaker in the world would do better than

the best if he gave each member of the audience an apple. Then the listener could feel it, see it, taste it, smell it, and hear it described—or hear it when he bites into it. He uses five senses.)

6. Speak from notes and a carefully structured outline; never read your speech. Keep your notes simple. Use three-by-five cards for your outline. This permits you to have eyeball-to-eyeball contact with your audience as you look at them and gauge their reactions. You can tell very quickly if an audience is interested or bored and restless. One of the worst speeches I ever heard was delivered by a general officer to my class at the Armed Forces Staff College. He had a teleprompter in front of him (which incidentally and mercifully obscured him from his audience), and he read the speech, obviously prepared by someone else, in a monotone. He never once looked at us, and five minutes after the speech was over, I had no idea of what he had been talking about. To this day, I just remember what a lousy speech it was.

7. Build to a major point, a climax, a pinnacle; and quit before the audience does. As George M. Cohan said, "Always leave them laughing." You may not necessarily leave them laughing, but you should leave them interested—wanting more.

8. Remember that you are not graded on the length of your speech but on its quality and content. Some of the best speeches (or sermons) have been only five or ten minutes long.

9. Finally, remember not to orate or preach; be yourself. Relax and your audience relaxes with you.

With proper preparation and a complete knowledge of the subject, you should have great confidence in yourself and be able to speak to your audience with authority, clarity, and humor.

Officers at all levels are required to make speeches or give briefings. When I was an instructor in the Airborne Department at Fort Sill, I gave one lecture in conjunction with the British liaison officer stationed there. He gave a polished, smooth, fact-filled lecture. I asked him later how he had managed to do so well on the platform on his very first try. He said that in the British Army young officers are constantly giving instructions to their troops or otherwise having to appear before an audience and speak. (I found out later it was a little more than that; the British very carefully selected their "brightest and best" for duty with the U.S. Army.)

It is also true that in the U.S. Army our officers are constantly being called upon to give speeches, lectures, instructions, and briefings. And the more senior you get, the more often you will be called upon to stand up and speak. When you are asked to make a speech, try to make a habit of using some of the techniques just outlined. Eventually, the sequence will become second nature.

Throughout my career, I have been called upon often to make speeches. They have ranged from giving instruction to my battery in training, to lectures at the Artillery School, to presentations at the War College, to talks to women's groups, to innumerable speeches to Rotary Clubs, American Legions, and at Fourth of July ceremonies, to briefings in French and Spanish (I must admit I violated one of my own precepts here—I read the speeches in Spanish and stuck very close to the script in French), to briefings for congressmen and senior Department of the Army and Defense officials, including the Secretary of Defense. And I have been called upon to write speeches for senior officers. (I wrote one for COMUSMACV to give to a joint session of Congress; however, I recognized only one line in the final version.) This recitation is just to point out that a routine military career carries with it the requirement to make speeches.

I have a shoe box filled with three-by-five cards on which I have written outlines for the speeches I have given in more recent years. I've given one speech so often, "The Need for a Strong Military Establishment," that when called upon to give it yet another time I get out the cards, update the data, outline a new introduction for the new audience, and have at it.

The worst speech I gave was to a men's church group in Oakland, California. I made the mistake of introducing the speech with a series of irrelevant and apparently not very funny stories that left the audience bored and uninterested. I managed to gather them back later in the speech, but I had done a lot of damage with the introduction. A few days after the speech, I received a splendid letter from a wise older man who had heard the speech and chided me for the introduction. After all of my years on various platforms, I should certainly have known better.

So, now you know how to give a speech and how not to do it.

Next time you get a speaking assignment, get out the cards, make your logical outline, rehearse it for time, content, and flow, and then proceed with confidence and perseverance.

Be yourself, and you'll be a winner.

The unit that stays together—fights a helluva lot better.

Stability

During World War II, divisions were formed from the cadres of already existing divisions, and the ranks were filled by the draftees out of the training centers. Once a man was assigned to a unit, he was usually there for the duration. There were exceptions, of course: OCS, other cadres, and, once in combat, wounds and sickness took men out of their original outfits. But, by and large, a man could count on being in the same unit with the same buddies until the war was over. And once his unit went overseas, it, too, was there for the duration.

The advantages of such stability are obvious: Men get to know one another well; they know their strengths, faults, and warts; they know their officers and NCOs; but most importantly, they form a unit bond that can be achieved in no other way—not with money, not with material comforts, not with gimmicks. And because of this closeness, this camaraderie, this caring for one another, men would sacrifice their own lives in combat to save a friend or help a unit. In his book *Goodbye, Darkness*, William Manchester dwells on the theme of unit cohesion. He talks about the "raggedy ass Marines," their inseparability, their devotion to one another, their sacrifices for each other. He portrays vividly how, in combat in the Pacific, these men became closer than "any friends had been or ever would be."

Many studies of war have proved conclusively that men fight and die, not for medals, not for glory, not for passes, but for their buddies and their outfit. And men get that closeness only through association with one another over a long period.

In the late, unlamented war in Vietnam, there were many personnel policy idiosyncrasies, not the least of which was the one-year tour and the six-months' command policy. Such policies absolutely guaranteed unit turmoil and precluded men from getting to know their fellow unit members intimately. The glue of cohesiveness formed by stability was lost.

The military must recognize the need for unit stability. Even at the lowest levels, a commander must strive within his power to keep his unit and subunits intact. He should stabilize his squads, sections, and platoons. The Army has seen some of the light and is attempting to ensure cohesiveness through its Cohort Program. May it be a success.

One has only to read about the hundreds of World War II unit reunions around the United States to recognize the validity and the value of unit stability, a unit forged in training, in battle, on passes, in foreign cities and towns. At any unit reunion, you cannot find a man who thought that his outfit was anything but the best, the elite, the saviors of the entire world.

This is a theme that must guide us in the future. It is basic to military personnel policies and management. Personnel are people, not abstract serial numbers spewing out of computers onto impersonal printout sheets. We can manage budgets and money that way; budgets and money have no feelings, no kindred relationships, no pride, no hopes. But soldiers *do*.

> But we . . . shall be remembered;
> We few, we happy few, we band of brothers;
> For he to-day that sheds his blood with me
> Shall be my brother; be he ne'er so vile
> This day shall gentle his condition.
>
> *Henry V,* Act IV, scene iii

This is why we have courts of law.

Story, Two Sides of

If there is one verity that becomes an article of faith as one progresses through any walk of life, and that bears repeating over and over, it is that there are always two sides to a story. Many arguments would never have started, countless altercations would have been smoothed, and innumerable difficulties would have been eased if both sides had stopped to consider the other side of the dispute.

Sometimes a commander, manager, or other person in authority will hear the so-called facts on one side of an incident and then, because he thinks that his subordinate's solution to the problem is cut and dried, will act accordingly. But very few matters are really that obvious, and ordinarily, there is time available to spend a few minutes to hear the other side of the story before making a decision.

(In combat, of course, the importance of knowing both sides of a situation, yours and the enemy's, is enormous and total. Whole courses at our service schools are devoted to this thesis. Therefore, the combat case simply goes without saying.)

As one illustration of this principle, knowing both sides of a story, I can offer the predicament of a soldier at Fort Riley. I was post commander at the time. At Riley, troops who were in the stockade (the stockade may now be called a correctional training facility or some such euphemism) were detailed to work around the post at sundry tasks. On this occasion, I spotted a prisoner who looked very soldierly and was working quite hard at his job—policing a road. I stopped to talk to him to find out why such an apparently good soldier was serving time in the stockade. He told me that he had gone AWOL because, even though he had applied for a leave, his company commander had turned him down rather perfunctorily. He had tried again with no success. Nor could he get

194

the first sergeant or his platoon leader to listen to why he needed leave. So he went AWOL. His girlfriend was giving birth to his child shortly, and he wanted to marry her before the event. I certainly don't commend the conduct that got the soldier in that uncomfortable predicament in the first place, but I do advocate a commander's taking the time to hear a soldier's story. The young trooper might have been saved the onus of a busted career and a tour in the stockade.

Another example of not investigating both sides of a situation occurred when I assumed command of a battery of the 11th Airborne Division in New Guinea. Prior to assuming command, the battalion commander told me to straighten it out forthwith, that it was the worst battery in Division Artillery, and so on. I started by relieving the first sergeant who, according to rumors and small talk of the battalion junior officers, was worthless and the major cause of the battery's unfortunate reputation. I did not give him a chance to prove himself with me, a new commander, and to this day I regret having summarily relieved him without giving him a fighting chance. I took the easy way out. He may have been worthless, but I never found out for myself.

Another instance wherein I did not know the full story involved a young, married lieutenant in my battalion. We had returned from combat in Korea a few months previously and were settling in to life at our permanent base in Kyushu, Japan. I suspected rather strongly that the lieutenant in question was living with a comely Japanese girl who was a waitress at the Officers' Club. Did I discuss the situation with the lieutenant? No. Did he talk to me about it? I didn't give him a chance. Did I talk to the waitress? Yes. Did she verify it? Yes. Was she lying? I don't know. I had the lieutenant transferred back to Korea in about a week. I suppose I had heard only one and a half sides of that story. Perhaps if I had talked to the lieutenant, he might have had an entirely different version. But I can't imagine what could have exonerated him.

One might listen to both sides of a story and then still, perhaps, make the wrong decision. For example, in May 1953, the 187th Airborne Regimental Combat Team was deployed to South Korea to bolster the U.N. Forces. The regiment went into reserve, but my artillery battalion was ordered to move up to add firepower to the defenses just south of the Iron Triangle, an area through which the U.N. Command expected at any hour a heavy frontal attack from the Chinese massed in the area. After I moved my firing batteries into position, I went forward to the infantry unit we were supporting to check on my forward observers. Because we were behind an infantry regiment from another unit, there were still a number of forward observers with them who were not from my battalion. I looked them over carefully and noted one young lieutenant who seemed particularly apprehensive. I thought nothing more about it until the next day when the lieutenant showed up at my battalion CP. He was visibly shaken. He told me that he could no longer stay with the company to which he was assigned, that he was afraid; he had a wife and two children back in Pennsylvania, and he blabbered on about the fact that he was not brave like the paratroopers in my battalion. He pleaded not to be sent back on line. I finally stopped him and permitted him to go back to his own artillery unit and not to his forward observer post. Did I make the right decision? I don't know. I do know that if I had forced him to go back on the hill that he had left, we would probably have had to court-martial him. I suppose I rationalized that he had some sort of battle fatigue and that he should be relieved. Besides that, I wanted to get my own forward observers in place. That does not answer the basic question of whether or not I did the right thing in that young fellow's case, but I did hear both sides of that story.

Essentially, the whole point of trying to find out both sides of a story before one makes a decision is to be as fair and just with the lives and careers of one's officers and soldiers as one can be. There are times when punishment is obviously justified, but it should be meted out only when one has all the facts. We are often victimized by hearing only one side. The culprit in any given situation is obviously going to make his side of the story benefit him as much as possible. He may not lie, but he may very well omit, distort, downplay, or otherwise camouflage facts to the distinct detriment of the opposition. I know that I am not alone when I say that many times I have been taken in by a smooth-talking soldier.

Certainly there is a point of no return. One can investigate and investigate, perhaps subconsciously to avoid making a decision. That is the obvious pitfall. One must avoid delays. But a slight delay to get all the facts is far better than making a hasty decision that is wrong and may have to be retracted.

Of all the principles of leadership, this one, that there are two sides to every story, is near the top of the list in importance.

Another busted link in the chain of command.

Stovepipe

Stovepiping is an arrangement whereby a certain function is controlled virtually from top to bottom through one organization, bypassing the normal chain of command. Our medical organization is an example of a stovepipe arrangement. So are our post exchanges, our commissaries, our communications, increasingly so our club system, our CID organization, our personnel management, and a number of other functional areas. The danger inherent in any stovepipe organization is that it bypasses the normal chain of command and thus deprives a commander of his authority over a function that affects his troops or his installation.

Sometimes a stovepipe arrangement is beneficial, as it is in the case of the post exchanges, which are run essentially by the Army and Air Force Exchange Service from its headquarters in Dallas. (Perhaps I think so because for a time I was the chairman of the Board of Directors of AAFES.) But one must recognize that the post exchanges today are a far cry from the sutlers of old who followed the troops around and sold them provisions varying from tobacco, to rum, to—well, what else is there?

The WW II exchanges at some training posts were one-room shacks that sold tobacco, toilet articles, and some magazines, for the most part. The centralization of the AAFES has permitted the sale of a vast variety of items at reduced prices while at the same time generating profits—$50 million one year while I was on the board—for troop recreational facilities such as marinas, bowling alleys, and racketball courts, day room furniture and subscriptions, theaters, and a variety of improved exchange facilities including shopping malls at our larger installations.

Strategic communications are undoubtedly best run through a vertical organization. But as more and more inroads are made on the authority of the commander—often without relieving him of the responsibility—the stovepipe organization could prove most detrimental to an efficient organization. It is another step in the centralization of command that, because of our instantaneous communication these days, permits the senior headquarters of the Department of Defense to control the lowest levels.

One of our greatest needs is to take the opposite tack and decentralize, to give authority back to the lowest possible levels of the command.

I include these comments for battalion and lower commanders for a couple of reasons: *(a)* to make them aware of the situation; *(b)* to forewarn them of the inherent problems of stovepiping; and *(c)* to suggest that, within their present and future power, they try to fend off stovepiping within their own units and to decentralize through the chain to the maximum.

Taking Charge, A Guide to

The February 25, 1980, issue of *Time* contained an article about Charles Knight, at forty-four one of the youngest chairmen of a major U.S. corporation. Emerson Electric, which he heads, is on many short lists of the best-managed companies in the country; his leadership must, therefore, be effective. Charles Knight's leadership rules consist of ten basic ingredients, some of which, he concedes, are obvious and corny. But I was struck with *(a)* the similarity of his precepts to those that I have heard preached throughout my military career and *(b)* their applicability at the lower levels of command. So, here they are—a very compelling list:

No. 1: You have to be able to set priorities. I always remember my father said, "Chuck, your health comes first; without that you have nothing. The family comes second. Your business comes third. You better recognize and organize those first two, so that you can take care of the third."

No. 2: You need an ability to grab hold of tough problems and not delegate them. It's not fair to let the guy below you take the brunt of making the hard decisions. The leader has to get deeply, personally involved in challenging issues and set the policy.

No. 3: Set and demand standards of excellence. Anybody who accepts mediocrity—in school, on the job, in life—is a guy who compromises. And when the leader compromises, the whole damn organization compromises.

No. 4: You need a sense of urgency. It is absolutely better to do something, recognizing that it may not be the right thing, than do nothing at all. If you don't have a sense of urgency, the bottom drops out of the organization.

No. 5: Pay attention to details. Getting the facts is the key to good decision making. Every mistake that I made—and we all make mistakes—came because I didn't take the time, I didn't drive hard enough, I wasn't smart enough to get the facts. You can't get them all, of course, but the last 5 or 10 percent of the facts may not really matter. [They might in a combat situation.]

No. 6: You need commitment. You can always pick out the guy who has a commitment. He is the fellow who does not fly into town on the morning of the meeting but flies in the night before to make sure that he gets there.

No. 7: Don't waste your time worrying about things you cannot do anything about. Don't try to fix things that are impossible. Concentrate on the possibles.

No. 8: You need the ability to fail. I'm amazed at the number of organizations that set up an environment where they do not permit their people to be wrong. You cannot innovate unless you are willing to accept some mistakes.

No. 9: Be tough but fair with people. Being tough means setting standards and demanding performance. Probably the hardest part of leadership is to make sure that you will not compromise when choosing people. You cannot let emotions get in the way when making a choice.

No. 10: You can't accomplish anything unless you're having some fun. Of course, it is clear that I have fun on the job. I get to the office every morning between 6:30 and 7:30. The other executives know that, so they try to get in the office early too. I hope they are having fun.

I would add an eleventh: Do the hardest job first. That pertains to strategy (the Allies in World War II decided that they would defeat the Axis—the stronger of the enemies—before launching an all-out offensive against Japan) as well as tactics; it pertains to everyday problem solving and decision making from large to small.

There you have it—a pretty good list to work from, even though the first ten come from a civilian.

For better or worse, there they are.

Telephones

The telephone is an instrument to be both praised and damned: Praised because it saves time, it is widely available, and it gives an intimacy that a letter does not; damned, because it provides no permanent record of the conversation (unless you're a high-level type who has a recorder attached to his phone), it interrupts one's chain of thought when it rings, and it can be a time-waster for long-winded conversationalists who can't get to the point.

There are a few rules that can help master the beast:

1. Place your own calls if possible. The higher your rank, the more important this is (provided you don't have to waste a lot of time getting the call through). The beauty of placing your own call, especially if you are calling someone junior to you, is that it goes through pretty fast and there is no jockeying between the secretaries about which boss is going to pick up the phone first.

2. Speak directly to the person you want. This eliminates the middleman and cuts down on the garbled messages that a middleman invariably produces—particularly if you are of fairly high rank (the higher one's rank, the more embellishment gets put on even relatively minor requests or comments).

3. Make memos for a record of your calls (if they are important) right after you have made or received the call. This eliminates confusion about who said what to whom.

4. Return calls as promptly as possible.

5. Particularly on long-distance calls, make some notes of what you are going to talk about before you place the call. Obviously, this shortens the call and saves time and money.

6. When all else fails and you need to get some cerebral work done, move to another office or unplug the gadget.

Naturally, the above rules pertain to a peacetime, noncombat environment. In combat, you must be always in communication up and down. I have heard some marvelous stories told of commanders who deliberately, but with great risk, "lose" communications with their higher headquarters when they want no interference, countermanding orders, or trivia to interfere with their operations. This is admirable if it works—foolhardy if it doesn't.

Well, there the telephone sits. It's not going to go away, so you might as well tame it.

Three-by-Five Cards

Along with the ballpoint pen and the pocket calculator, three-by-five cards must rank with the greatest assets known to an action officer, commander, NCO, or PFC. The cards are ubiquitous, useful, cheap, alphabetizable, and beautifully sized for any number of brain- and memory-helping tasks. Here are a few for which I have used them over the years:

1. Shirt-pocket stuffer. Along with a ballpoint pen, three-by-five cards clipped together fit nicely in the upper left pocket of a shirt. They are then handy for jotting down anything that comes to mind—a phone call to make, a list of things to be done, observations, comments, an endless myriad of items.

2. Speech cards. Whenever I give a speech, I have the outline on three-by-five cards, which permits me to shuffle them as necessary, add to points as I go over the outline, use quotes in the proper places, add or subtract from the speech conveniently, and keep them in a pocket unobtrusively until speech time.

3. Files of all sorts. This includes addresses, telephone numbers, statistics, memos for record, quotes, ideas, projects, short personnel files—the list goes on and on. They can be easily alphabetized for easy reference.

4. Reminders. Write what you want to remember on a three-by-five card and stick it in your calendar if it has a suspense date; if not, just put it in a desk drawer with others to be reviewed periodically.

There are probably as many uses for the three-by-five card as there are users of the things. In going through my desk today, I find that I have assorted cards doing many things: speech outlines, as I've already mentioned; one box full of cards, alphabetized, with notes I made as Deputy CG of Eighth Army in Korea, ranging from

"Army Audit Agency" and "Armed Forces Korea Network" to "Maintenance" to "Oerlikon 35mm AA Guns" to "President Ford's Visit" to "Yom Kippur War, Lessons From"; stories; quotes; and a whole stack of cards containing notes I made in Vietnam while traveling with the Deputy COMUSMACV; ideas for articles I intend to write (that stack is about three inches thick); articles I have written and have had published or are at a publisher (the reject stack is also pretty thick); and another box full of cards with addresses and phone numbers of various friends and acquaintances.

Thus, for us of normal intelligence and memory capacity, three-by-five cards are godsends.

Get organized: Don't waste it.

Time

Many items in this book try to explain how to do things better and quicker and are, therefore, about time. But there is one important point about time itself. When do you do your best work—morning, afternoon, or at night?

As you grow in experience, you realize that your most productive hours may be bunched at either end of the day and are rarely spread evenly throughout the day. You may find that you like to get up at five in the morning and do your hard and/or thinking work in the early hours. Someone else may find that regime a ridiculous affront to his inner mechanism and far prefer the late hours of the day or even night for his cogitation, hard work, and problem solving.

Whatever your inner functions tell your brain, the point is clear: Find out for yourself when it is that you are most productive, and schedule your time accordingly.

In peacetime, this is all there is.

Training

Many volumes have been published on the subject of training: how to do it, who's responsible, where it should be done, and how it should be done. In Europe in 1966, as USAREUR was being drawn down to support our forces in Vietnam, a great problem developed in the training of the divisions still left in Europe. The European divisions were reduced greatly in strength and were fairly well disorganized because of the constant personnel turnover, short tours, and fragmented units. The commander in Europe at the time decided that, when the replacements started coming in, he would fill up one unit at a time rather than spread the replacements on an even level throughout the command. Thus, a squad was filled, then its platoon, then its company, then its battalion. This meant, of course, that men would have more time to train together and to get to know one another, and it resulted in stability and cohesiveness throughout the command.

This system of filling by small unit indirectly emphasized one of the essentials of a good training policy: Training must be done by unit or under that unit's commander. Trainers must emphasize the small unit first, the squad, the gun crew, the tank crew. With those units well trained, it is simple to put the building blocks together and make an efficient, well-trained division.

In Germany, we who were used to large division- and even corp-sized posts in the United States, were struck by the fact that German barracks rarely housed more than a regiment. Aditionally, their training areas were of necessity small and cramped. How, then, could the Germans have trained the many divisions, corps, and larger units that performed so brutally and effectively in the early years of World War II? The answer lay in the fact that the Germans trained their smaller units (battalions and regiments) to perfection and then, for combat, put them together to form smoothly operating divisions. There are many lessons to be learned from that system.

Training need not be stereotyped. To this day, I remember a demonstration I set up for my parachute artillery battery while we were still training in New Guinea. My battery was pretty well drilled by that time in field artillery techniques, and feeling that when we got into combat we might fight as infantry (which, as it turned out, happened to almost all the 11th Airborne artillery units except my battery), I asked a classmate infantry company commander to send over one of his squads to demonstrate infantry tactics. The squad ran through a squad attack problem on the football field behind our battery tents using a 55-gallon drum as the objective. The demonstration pointed out the similarity of squad tactics to football tactics and gave my battery a very clear understanding of flanking attacks, field of fire, base of fire, and fire and movement. Simple but precise and pertinent demonstrations have a way of staying with one for a long time; I've remembered this one since 1944.

Training must emphasize the small unit, for a unit is equal in quality only to the sum of the quality of its subordinate parts. You can't possibly have a good battalion without having good platoons, and it seems to me that with air/land battle 2000 tactics, the small unit becomes even more vital to success on the battlefield.

This lesson of small unit training is obviously particularly pertinent to company- and battalion-sized units. Commanders at those levels can emphasize unit training under their own commanders, can set up competitions between units, and can watch with some pride as the small units gradually fuse together into one smooth working command.

Uniforms

During my career in the Army, we went through a wide variety of uniforms—both combat and dress. When I was at West Point (1939–1943), the instructors wore pinks and greens with Sam Browne belts. Some of the more dashing cavalry types wore pink riding breeches and highly polished Peal boots. Officers wore form-fitting, beltless, almost shin-length Horstmann overcoats of a very heavy tan material that had a slit at the waist for attaching one's saber to the Sam Browne belts on the inside. During World War II, we wore pinks and greens (but by then without the Sam Browne belts) and a cut-off, belted version of the Horstmann overcoat. By the end of the war, we had cut off our blouses to emulate the battle dress of the Brits. Then, during the Korean War, the whole Army went to an OD dress uniform with the cut-off, so-called Eisenhower jacket. Finally, we went to the all-green uniform. (During the whole period, however, the white, blue dress, and blue mess uniform remained unchanged except for material, blue uniform insignias, and pants' stripes.)

In the overcoat department, I can count personal ownership of at least six different versions; jackets for outerwear, at least four; summer uniforms, three or four; hats, at least eight; combat uniforms, from jumpsuits, to heavy fatigues with the sleeves rolled down for fighting in the Philippines, to wool uniforms for combat in Europe, to one-piece coveralls for jump training in 1943, to jungle fatigues for Vietnam, to today's camouflaged fatigues. We had sweaters for wear *under* our fatigues and wool combat uniforms but not the so-called woolly-pully for *outer* wear prevalent in today's Army.

Enlisted men's uniforms went through even more frequent and radical changes. Their insignia of rank changed sizes and colors and

209

went from their sleeves to their collars and back to their sleeves and, in today's version, to shoulder boards. Their combat uniforms followed the vagaries of the officers'.

After wearing and watching the changing styles of uniforms over the years, I feel compelled to ask a few questions:

1. Why have we gone to such an outlandish uniform for outerwear as the woolly-pully sweater with shoulder boards on the outside?

2. Why do enlisted men wear shoulder boards? It's hard enough to tell the difference in dress between an officer and an EM as it is.

3. Why don't we stick to the tried and true uniforms that make men look like soldiers? (Pinks and greens are *still* the best-looking general wear uniform of the past three generations of officers.)

4. Why have we gone to a sack overcoat without belt even as the civilian population is going to the traditional military trench coat?

5. In short, why are we tinkering with something that isn't broken? (I'll admit that the heavy fatigues of World War II were unsuited for jungle fighting and that the camouflage fatigues of today's Army are a step in the right direction, although the troops who went into Grenada found plenty of fault with their camouflaged fatigues.)

This chapter really has no bearing on the decisions or actions of NCOs and junior officers. I include it out of nostalgia and so that today's officers and NCOs might have some idea of the uniform changes during the post–World War II period. A few years ago a young colonel (now a young brigadier general) asked me what "pinks and greens" were. Though I shouldn't have been, I was surprised *(a)* that an officer could get to be a full colonel without having been in the "pink and green" Army and *(b)* that I was old enough and had been around the Army long enough to be able to tell him.

While I am on the subject of uniforms, I want to take a bit of credit for how the stateside Army got to roll its fatigue sleeves up. I returned from nineteen months in Vietnam in 1968 to command the Special Warfare Center (later the John F. Kennedy Center for Military Assistance) at Fort Bragg. In Vietnam, we habitually wore our jungle fatigue sleeves rolled up unless there was a good reason to the contrary—excessive bugs, for example. At any rate, the summers at Fort Bragg were hot, and it seemed to me only reasonable and eminently justifiable that the troops should be permitted to roll up their fatigue sleeves. And since my command was in the same jungle fatigues that we had worn in Vietnam (and, I believe, the only unit in the United States at the time so uniformed), it seemed even more logical and humane. Therefore, I wrote a letter to the Department of the Army suggesting that my command—naturally, I always figured that my command was the best and the most deserving—be permitted to roll up the sleeves of its jungle fatigues during the summer months.

The letter found its way to a friend of mine who had been a brigade commander in Vietnam and was familiar with the problems of the troops in the field. But, he suggested, he couldn't do it only for the Special Forces, and he couldn't do it for the Army as a whole. The United States has many different climates and problems. Well, I countered, why not put out an Army policy that the sleeves be up or down at the discretion of the post or major unit commander? Well, he liked that idea, and within about two weeks, an incredibly short time for a DA policy to wend its way through the halls of the Pentagon and find its way to the troops in the field, we were permitted to roll up sleeves at the discretion of the local commander. I'm sure that the Special Forces were the first to inaugurate that policy. But I know of one post commander in South Carolina who took about two years to make the decision.

There are all kinds of stories—some real, some fanciful—about how uniform decisions are made. One involved Gen. Maxwell Taylor and the black stripes on the trousers of officers' green uniforms. General Taylor, when Chief of Staff, allegedly heard a briefing on the new green uniform and personally decided then and there that officers would have a wide stripe down their trouser legs and generals would have two narrow ones.

Then there's the tale of how the G.I. belt buckle went from brass to black, if only for a short time. The deputy chief of staff for Logistics, not really in the business of making decisions about uniforms, heard a briefing in his office on the new green uniform. It was up to him to procure it. He saw the uniform modeled, realized that the shoes were going from brown to black, that the socks were going to be black, and that the belt was going from tan to black. As the briefing team was leaving his office, the DCSLOG shouted after them: ''And while you're at it, make the buckle black, too.''

I'm certain that as long as the Army hierarchy is staffed with people who have tastes of their own, they will have ideas of how the Army should be dressed. They will continue to tinker with the Army uniform. (Maternity fatigues? God forbid.) And as more and exotic cloths make their way into the clothing business, there will be more and more opportunity for change. Some, like the jungle fatigues, will be good; others, like the all-purpose sack coats passing for military overcoats, will be bad. But maybe, with luck, we'll average out ahead. Now if the Nadick Laboratory experts could develop a decent combat boot . . .

War

There is many a boy here to-day who looks on war as all glory, but, boys, it is all hell.

> William Tecumseh Sherman
> Address, GAR Convention
> Columbus, Ohio
> August 11, 1880

I am sick and tired of war. Its glory is all moonshine. It is only those who have neither fired a shot nor heard the shrieks and groans of the wounded who cry aloud for blood, more vengeance, more desolation. War is hell.

> William Tecumseh Sherman
> Graduation Speech, Michigan
> Military Academy
> June 19, 1879

> God and the soldier, we adore
> In time of danger, not before;
> The danger passed, and all things righted,
> God is forgotten, and the soldier slighted.
>
> One of Marlborough's veterans

Someone remarked to Napoleon that "God is always on the side of the largest battalions." "Nothing of the kind," said Napoleon. "Providence is always on the side of the last reserve."

War is one of the constants of history and has not diminished with civilization or democracy. In the last 3,421 years of recorded history, only 268 have seen no war.

> Will and Ariel Durant
> *The Lessons of History*

For a war to be just three conditions are necessary—public authority, just cause, right motive.

> St. Thomas Aquinas
> *Summa Theologica*

We don't want any more wars, but a man is a damn fool to think that there won't be any more of them. I am a peace-loving Quaker, but when war breaks out every damn man in my family goes. If we're ready, nobody will tackle us . . .

> Smedley Butler
> *The World Tomorrow*
> October 1931

There's no use talking about abolishing war; that's damn foolishness. Take the guns away from men and they will fight just the same.

> Ibid.

Once we have a war there is only one thing to do. It must be won. For defeat brings worse things than any that can ever happen in war.

> Ernest Hemingway
> *Men at War*

It is vain, sir, to extenuate the matter. The gentlemen may cry, Peace, peace! but there is no peace. The war has actually begun! The next gale that sweeps from the north will bring to our ears the clash of resounding arms! Our brethren are already in the field! Why stand we here idle? What is it that the gentlemen wish? What would they have? Is life so dear or peace so sweet as to be purchased at the price of chains and slavery? Forbid it, Almighty God. I know not what course others may take, but as for me, give me liberty or give me death!

> Patrick Henry
> Speech on the Stamp Act
> Virginia Convention
> March 23, 1775

I am insulted by the persistent assertion that I want war. Am I a fool? War! It would settle nothing.

> Adolf Hitler
> Interview with *Le Matin*
> November 10, 1933

War is our business. I include these quotes because they are about our profession. It does our young officers and NCOs good to pause and mull over in their minds the vagaries of their calling, to realize that over the centuries wars have been part of civilization, and to know that their chosen profession is vital for the country and transcends in importance any other occupation or calling.

There is no substitute for victory.

Douglas MacArthur

Briefings, Fort Riley, Kansas. U.S. Army photo

Keep it down.

Weight

Overweight in grade, obesity, fatness—whatever it is called—marks a man or woman, in perception if not in reality, as one who is out of shape, incapable of doing prolonged, fatiguing work, undisciplined, and a poor model for younger soldiers and officers.

The importance of your weight to your career was brought home forcefully to me every time I sat on a promotion board—of which occasions there were many, including the highest level board, the one selecting generals for permanent promotion to major general. (After that, no promotion boards; the Secretary of the Army and the Chief of Staff do their own selecting for three- and four-star generals. And there is no permanent rank above major general.)

On one particular occasion, we were selecting colonels for promotion to brigadier general. One of the top-notch, outstanding files belonged to a colonel who commanded a brigade in my division. The colonel had survived the process all the way to the last hundred or so. (We had been directed to select fifty-five.) But the going gets rough at the end of the selection process, and the board has to pass over superior men to get to the final select group. The colonel in question did not make the final cut because his picture in his file showed a man somewhat overweight. When I returned to the division, I talked to the colonel and told him that he had to lose about twenty pounds and submit a new picture to DA—one of a more streamlined, svelte colonel, him, no one else. He did so and made the selection for brigadier on the next list. Today he is a relatively slender four-star general.

Aside from appearance, however, overweight can be a serious health hazard and a detriment to enjoying life to the fullest. There's been enough said on that subject without the need for me to expound on it further. Suffice it to say that in the military, above all other professions, men must stay in shape throughout their entire careers. No other profession (well, maybe professional athletics for a shorter time) puts such a demand on physical fitness and stamina as does the military. There is nothing more strenuous, blood-pressure raising, or injurious to one's health than combat. Those who enter it in poor physical condition are raising their odds for nonsurvival. That's the most important reason for a soldier to stay slim. And it is the duty of the chain of command—particularly at the lower end—to see to it that their units are fit to fight.

The 5.2 mile run. U.S. Army photo

Duty, Honor, Country.

West Point

Probably there can be no more controversial a subject than what West Point is, should be, or used to be. A graduate, no matter how old, who criticizes the present administration for real or imagined shortcomings (e.g., cadets stripping to the waist on national TV at the Army-Navy game; different standards for athletes than for other cadets; relaxation of discipline; elimination of traditions, tenth system in academics, and plebe system; voluntary meals; strolling to class; women in the Corps; civilian clothes on the Plain; beer in the cadet lounges, etc.) is ridiculed as an "old fool," die-hard, "The Corps has gone to Hell" type. Nonetheless, and with full knowledge that I am a reactionary who would try to turn back the clock, I'll take a crack at what I think West Point should be.

First, it should be, in fact, a seminary not only teaching subjects that have specific application to a career in the Army but also molding a cadet's entire psyche to service to the country, honorable, and duty-bound. Second, West Point academics should stress mathematics and the physical sciences, military history, English (for four years, not two), one foreign language (again, four years, not two), military law, geography, and political science. The social sciences and psychology should be left to the tactical officers from whom cadets in other days learned the precepts of leadership, conduct, and personal values that lasted them throughout a lifetime of service. Third, the life of a cadet should be spartan, disciplined, and totally military. When a man enters West Point, he is following a vocation, not just a four-year tour at just another college.

If West Point is something other than this, if it is just another second-rate engineering school (as even some civilians recently have characterized it), then there is simply no need for it. It costs too much.

There are many good engineering schools throughout the country; there are many good ROTC programs to turn out officers; but there should be and can be only one West Point—steeped in memorable traditions, dedicated to producing career soldiers, uncompromising with the ideals, dedication, and excellence that have produced great military and civilian leaders from the time of its inception. No other educational institution in this country can boast of graduates who have achieved so much.

So let us stop tinkering with West Point. Let us not be confused about its mission. Let us not forget the values set by General MacArthur in his unforgettable, monumental farewell address to the Corps of Cadets at West Point:

> Yours is the profession of arms, the will to win, the sure knowledge that in war there is no substitute for victory, that if you lose, the Nation will be destroyed, that the very obsession of your public service must be duty, honor, country.
>
> Others will debate the controversial issues, national and international, which divide men's minds. But serene, calm, aloof, you stand as the Nation's war guardian, as its lifeguard from the raging tides of international conflict, as its gladiator in the arena of battle. For a century and a half you have defended, guarded, and protected its hallowed traditions of liberty, of freedom, of right and justice.
>
> Let civilian voices argue the merits or demerits of our processes of government: Whether our strength is being sapped by deficit financing indulged in too long, by Federal paternalism grown too mighty, by power groups grown too arrogant, by politics grown too corrupt, by crime grown too rampant, by morals grown too low, by taxes grown too high, by extremists grown too violent; whether our personal liberties are as thorough and complete as they should be.
>
> These great national problems are not for your professional participation or military solution. Your guideposts stand out like a tenfold beacon in the night: Duty, Honor, Country.
>
> You are the leaven which binds together the entire fabric of our national system of defense.
>
> From our ranks come the great captains who hold the Nation's destiny in their hands the moment the war tocsin sounds.
>
> The long gray line has never failed us. Were you to do so, a million ghosts in olive drab, in brown khaki, in blue and gray, would rise from their white crosses, thundering those magic words: Duty, Honor, Country.

The words of General MacArthur are as applicable to non-West Pointers in the Army as they are to graduates. They pertain to all officers—OCS graduates, ROTC products, direct commissions. His is the voice of experience, clarity, and wisdom. He was a phenomenal success in the military, and his words demand attention. Hear him and heed him.

West Point today

Bless 'em all, Bless 'em all,
the long and the short and the tall . . .

Wives

Two events in recent years have highlighted Army wives in situations of excruciating pain, made the more difficult because, while undergoing their shock, they were subjected to the glare of worldwide publicity and total media coverage. The Army wives were Mrs. Ray, whose husband was gunned down on the streets of Paris, and Mrs. Dozier, whose husband was seized by Italian terrorists, an act to which she was a witness. Mrs. Ray's loss was final; Mrs. Dozier has the comfort of her husband's almost miraculous rescue.

These two women vividly represent countless Army wives who have experienced, in private, equally painful personal losses and who have sacrificed so much for the men they married and the country that they serve. Army wives are truly unsung heroines. They spend lonely months rearing children while their husbands are away in wars, on short-tour overseas assignments, or, what seems equally long, weeks in the field on maneuvers or exercises. They raise their families in converted barracks, substandard housing, or inadequate and expensive houses off post. They commit themselves to the often austere life in the Army just as totally as do their husbands.

Even in so-called normal, peacetime post life, Army wives of officers and NCOs are called upon to spend countless hours doing volunteer work for the many agencies that bind the post and the Army units together: Red Cross, Army Community Service, Thrift Shop, youth activities, churches, and the many other clubs and groups that do generous and splendid work for Army families.

The higher the rank of an NCO or an officer, the more is expected of his wife. She is awakened at 0300 by phone calls from distraught wives; she runs car pools for soldiers' families without cars; she visits the sick in the hospitals; she mourns with other wives

221

who suffer disasters large and small, real and imagined. And through it all, one expects her to be calm, collected, in control. One rarely thinks that she has any problems of her own.

There is not enough praise to heap on the shoulders of this gallant, hard-working, and mostly anonymous group of women. From Molly Pitcher on, they have sacrificed, worked, and made do as they traveled from post to post and country to country.

God bless them all!

Army family symposium. U.S. Army photo, R. D. Ward

Summary

1. Listen to both sides of every story.
2. Be hard but fair and compassionate.
3. Give a man a job and let him do it.
4. Use the chain of command.
5. Know your job and your troops.
6. Praise in public, chew in private.
7. Set priorities.
8. Do the hardest job first.
9. Don't ask your troops to do something you cannot or would not do.
10. Set high standards.
11. Do it now; don't procrastinate.
12. Take care of the details.
13. Commit yourself totally to your job.
14. Take care of your troops.
15. Assign missions by unit.
16. Do your homework.
17. Get out and see what's going on.
18. Decentralize.
19. Trust your junior officers and NCO.
20. Eliminate as many boards, committees, councils, and special assistants as possible.
21. Keep your boss informed of bad news as well as good.
22. Emphasize precision, soldierly bearing, smartness in all ceremonies.

23. Don't try to be a "hail fellow, well met" with your subordinates.
24. Encourage competition among units.
25. Give credit where and when due.
26. Never give an order you can't enforce.
27. Be honest, fair, and objective on efficiency reports.
28. Follow up orders to make certain they're being carried out.
29. Keep the troops informed—but don't take votes.
30. Inspect all areas of your unit routinely.
31. Make the troops live like soldiers (spit and shine).
32. Learn another language.
33. Develop your writing and speaking skills.
34. Be as loyal to your troops as you expect them to be to you.
35. Continue your education, especially history and geography.
36. Keep in superb physical shape.
37. Understand your mission (and deadlines) completely before getting started.
38. Admit your mistakes; never try to cover up.
39. Never lie to your troops or your boss.
40. Relieve a man from his position only as a last resort.
41. Emphasize the small units (squad, section) in training.
42. Never punish an entire unit for the transgressions of an unknown few of its members; find the culprit or culprits and punish them.
43. If it ain't broke, don't fix it.

The Los Banos raid—a summary illustration.

Epilogue

This book deals with how to be successful. But so far, it hasn't talked much about "success at what?" Obviously, the mission of the Army is to be successful in combat. Each officer and NCO must strive to see to it that his unit is successful in combat. Thus, the success we talk about is not so much personal success as unit success. After that, personal success is measured in other ways, promotions, awards, more challenging commands, more demanding staff jobs. But the basic success for which one strives is the success of his unit in combat.

On February 23, 1945, a reinforced battalion of the 11th Airborne Division launched a highly successful raid against a Japanese internee camp some forty-two miles behind the lines southeast of Manila. The battalion launched the attack by land, sea, and air; the recon element came across the water by Laguna de Bay in native *bancas*; part of the assault force dropped in by parachute. The main body of the battalion boated across Laguna de Bay in huge, lumbering amphibious tractors, and a relief force moved overland by truck and by foot until halted by Japanese fire.

Perhaps none of this appears particularly noteworthy until one considers that *(a)* the units participating in the raid were pulled out of their fighting positions around Manila only five days before the attack, *(b)* the commander of the force that attacked the camp, a twenty-six-year-old major named Hank Burgess, CO of the 1st Battalion of the 511th Parachute Infantry, became involved in the planning for the raid only on February 18, *(c)* the commander of the fifty-nine Amtracs that transported the 1st Battalion, 511th Parachute Infantry Regiment (minus B Company, which jumped into the camp) was a full colonel under the command of the major commanding the raiding force, *(d)* headquarters higher than the 11th

Airborne's were not involved in any of the detailed planning and, as a matter of fact, were purposely given only scant information by the 11th about the raid until it was completed, *(e)* intelligence for the operation came not from satellite photos, radio intercepts, or other esoteric modern-day devices, but from two escaped internees, from rather crude aerial photos, but mostly from a nine-man squad from the division recon platoon that infiltrated the area and cased the camp by night, *(f)* prior to the raid, there was no written order, *(g)* the commander of the parachute element, 1st Lt. John B. Ringer, CO of B Company, 511th Parachute Regiment, first heard about his part in the raid on February 20, *(h)* intelligence estimated that there were some three hundred Japanese troops in and around the immediate vicinity of the camp and the Japanese 8th Division, some ten thousand men, was in position about eight miles from Los Banos, *(i)* the entire raiding force was the 1st Battalion, 511th (some 412 men) reinforced with two pack 75s from the 457th Parachute FA Battalion, *(j)* the force moving overland, the 188th Glider Regiment with two understrength battalions reinforced with some artillery, never got to the camp, and *(k)* the raiding force killed or neutralized some 240 Japanese guarding the camp, successfully evacuated 2,147 emaciated, starving, crippled internees and suffered not one casualty. The 188th, held up at a river crossing by the Japanese, lost two men killed and two wounded.

Maj. Hank Burgess, the overall commander of the raiding force, says that a successful raid requires the execution of three things: An undetected and secret approach march, the seizure and holding of the objective long enough to carry out the mission of the raid, and a withdrawal.

The Los Banos raid encompassed all three, of course. The approach march was made by two elements: B Company parachuting into the camp at 0700 on the 23d and the 1/511th hitting the beach in Amtracs at the same time; the seizure of the objective, the sixty acres of the camp, was executed by the division recon platoon reinforced with about forty-five local guerrillas which had infiltrated the area and attacked the guards as soon as the first parachute opened above them, and by B Company 1/511th once they were on the ground; the holding of the objective area was accomplished by the amphibious element that arrived shortly after the paratroops; and the withdrawal phase was performed by the entire battalion escorting and shuttling the internees in the Amtracs back across Laguna de Bay.

There can be no doubt that the Los Banos raid was a textbook model of a successful small unit operation. And so, as the instructors say in all the military classrooms, what were the lessons learned?

Here are a few:

1. The commander of the raiding force had a clear-cut mission, the support of the major command (the 11th Airborne Division), and the authority to plan and execute his mission with little outside guidance and interference.

2. The troops involved were highly trained, motivated, self-confident, self-assured, enthusiastic, and battle-tested.

3. Once the commander was on the objective, he had the authority to make decisions (including ordering a nervous full colonel with the Amtracs to postpone a premature departure).

4. The operation was decentralized to the commander on the ground, so much so that when a staff officer from a higher headquarters appeared unexpectedly over the area in an artillery spotter plane, the CO on the ground conveniently turned off his radio.

5. There was a minimum of administration involved; Major Burgess did not even have the usual five-paragraph field order before the operation; he had the Division G–3 work one up for posterity and higher headquarters' edification *after* the operation.

6. The chain of command worked—in this situation, it had to.

7. Communications outside the raid area were the barest minimum necessary.

8. The plan evolved from a critically important mission in which speed was essential to prevent further harm to the internees.

9. The planning followed the traditional and time-tested sequence in the estimate of the situation that resulted in a "go" decision.

And did it follow the principles of war? You bet it did. **Mass** at the point of decision; clear-cut, well-defined **objective**; complete **security** from higher headquarters; total **surprise** (the Japanese did not think we would hit and run behind their lines); **unity of command**—everything at the camp was under Major Burgess, including a full colonel's Amtrac battalion. It was definitely an **offensive** operation; the raiding force **(economy of force)** was properly tailored to accomplish the mission; the plan was **simple** and every man knew exactly what he was supposed to do.

Result: the combat operation was a resounding success from any standpoint.

And that's what this book has been about.